Edward Lear

Twayne's English Authors Series

Herbert Sussman, Editor
Northeastern University

TEAS 336

EDWARD LEAR
(1812–1888)
Copyright owned by

Edward Lear

By Ina Rae Hark
University of South Carolina, Columbia

Twayne Publishers • *Boston*

Edward Lear

Ina Rae Hark

Copyright © 1982 by G. K. Hall & Company
Published by Twayne Publishers
A Division of G. K. Hall & Company
70 Lincoln Street
Boston, Massachusetts 02111

Printed on permanent/durable
acid-free paper and bound in
The United States of America.

Library of Congress Cataloging in Publication Data

Hark, Ina Rae.
Edward Lear.

(Twayne's English authors series; TEAS 336)
Bibliography: p. 150
Includes index.
1. Lear, Edward, 1812-1888—Criticism
and interpretation. I. Title. II. Series.
PR4879.L2Z64 1982   821'.8   81-20039
ISBN 0-8057-6822-X   AACR2

To my parents,
Annette and Hershel Hark

Contents

About the Author

Ina Rae Hark received the B.A. from Northwestern University and the M.A. and Ph.D. from the University of California, Los Angeles. She is an Associate Professor in the Department of English at the University of South Carolina, Columbia, where she has taught film studies, Victorian literature, and modern drama since 1973. She has published articles on Cardinal Newman, Charles Dickens, G. B. Shaw, Samuel Butler, and several topics in film and popular culture. Dr. Hark is currently concentrating her research on Victorian satiric and comic literature.

Preface

Once, after I had finished lecturing to a graduate seminar on the ways Edward Lear's nonsense poems reflect the Victorian ambivalence about society's control of the individual, an earnest student, who had enjoyed Lear since childhood, protested the absurdity of reading such things into verse clearly intended as mere uncomplicated fun. Left unspoken, but strongly implied, was his conviction that I had fallen victim to the excessive pedantry of academic life.

Although this study and others that have preceded it make clear that there was nothing uncomplicated about either Lear or his works, it is true that much of a reader's enjoyment of them derives from a peculiar charm that defies analysis. When constructing critical models to apply to Dongs, Pobbles, and Quangle Wangles, I had, I must confess, moments when I felt it might be wiser to take the position of Sidney Colvin, who reviewed Lear's third nonsense book, *More Nonsense*, in the *Academy* on January 15, 1872. Colvin claimed that it was a "stout, jovial book" that "transcends criticism as usual"; he promised therefore only to indicate its contents briefly "and then leave the reader to his unmolested entertainment."

Because it is especially dangerous in the case of an artist like Lear that one might murder to dissect, I have attempted in the pages that follow never to reduce his nonsense to a single, bland "meaning" or to explain away what Thomas Byrom aptly designates as its "wonder." My primary purpose has been to show how strongly interconnected each work is with all the others, and how a reader will appreciate any one Lear verse or story according to how many others he has read. I treat all Lear's writings as a single work broken up into many small units.

Lear's experience of the world convinced him of life's unpredictability and arbitrary changefulness, qualities that generally worked to deprive the secure of security, to isolate the nonconformist from a place in the social order, even if he had not chosen his nonconformity, and to keep the loving from finding love. In the alternate world he created through his nonsense, he examined all the possible effects such a capricious universe could have on its inhabitants, including episodes of miraculous joy amid the more prevalent disappointments. No one poem presents Lear's total vision but each adds a piece to the puzzle. The following survey of the entire Lear oeuvre aims to put the pieces together without necessarily dictating a specific response to the completed design. In keeping with this approach, I have dealt with Lear's work by type—limericks, longer poems, miscellaneous nonsense forms—rather than taking a chronological view.

My interest in Lear began with my dissertation days at UCLA, and I would like to acknowledge the assistance of two members of my doctoral committee in launching my Learian researches. Ada Nisbet first advised me to include Lear in my study of Victorian "topsyturvydom," and my dissertation director, G. B. Tennyson, supervised the writing of my initial criticism of Lear. I would also like to thank the Twayne Victorian field editor, Herbert Sussman, for inviting me to do this study, my colleagues John Ower and Patrick Scott for reading parts of the book in draft form, Vivien Noakes for her prompt reply to my letter of inquiry, and Donna Miller and the secretarial staff in the English Department at the University of South Carolina for typing the manuscript.

Ina Rae Hark

University of South Carolina, Columbia

Chronology

1812   Edward Lear born May 12 at Bowman's Lodge, Holloway, the son of Jeremiah Lear, a stockbroker, and Ann Skerrett Lear. He is the twentieth of twenty-one children.

1816   Jeremiah Lear in financial difficulties. Family leaves Bowman's Lodge for a time, Lear entrusted to the care of his sister, Ann.

1817   Experiences first epileptic seizure.

1828   Begins life as a working artist, living with Ann off the Gray's Inn Road, doing anatomical and natural history sketches.

1832   Publishes *Illustrations of the Family of Psittacidae, or Parrots*. Invited to draw the menagerie of the Earl of Derby at Knowsley, where he works off and on for the next five years.

1833   Death of Lear's father.

1837   Leaves England to pursue a career as a traveling landscape painter. After passing through Belgium, Luxembourg, Germany, and Italy, he establishes a base in Rome.

1838–   Traveling and painting in southern Italy, with visits to
1848   England in 1841 and 1845.

1844   Death of Lear's mother.

1845   Meets Chichester Fortescue, later Lord Carlingford.

1846   *A Book of Nonsense* and *Gleanings from the Menagerie and Aviary at Knowsley Hall* published.

1848–   Meets Thomas Baring, later Lord Northbrook. In March
1849   1848 Lear leaves Italy because of the uncertain political climate and journeys through Greece, Turkey, Albania, the Ionian islands, Malta, and Egypt. In March 1849 he meets Franklin Lushington in Malta and travels with him throughout southern Greece. In June Lear returns to England and meets Alfred and Emily Tennyson. `

1850	Begins a ten-year painting course at the Royal Academy. Remains in England for three and a half years.
1851	*Journals of a Landscape Painter in Albania &c* published.
1852	Meets Holman Hunt and other Pre-Raphaelites, whose work he admires. *Journals of a Landscape Painter in Southern Calabria &c* published.
1853	Leaves England in December to travel in Egypt.
1854	After three-month sojourn in Egypt, returns to England via Malta and Marseilles. Goes on a walking tour of the Alps in the fall.
1855	Realizes that he can never settle in England to complete the Royal Academy course. In October he accompanies Lushington to Corfu and establishes a winter base there.
1856	Employs Giorgio Kokali, his Suliot manservant, who was to be with him for twenty-seven years. Meets Helena Cortazzi.
1857	Visits England from May to November.
1858	Expedition to the Near East, then back to Corfu and to England in August. Moves to Rome by year's end. Stays through May 1860 with an extended visit home from April to December 1859.
1861–	Enlarged edition of *Book of Nonsense* published 1861.
1864	Based on Corfu with summers and autumns in England. His sister Ann dies on March 11, 1861.
1862	"Romance" with Augusta Bethell begins.
1864	Leaves Corfu for England via Greece.
1865–	Travels extensively throughout Mediterranean area and
1867	Near East. Summers in England. Deepest involvement with Gussie in 1866, but Lear leaves for Egypt and Palestine without making his intended proposal.
1867–	Living in Cannes, visiting England in the summer and
1868	fall of 1867 and Corsica in April 1868.
1869	Meets Hubert Congreve in San Remo, Italy.
1870	Living in Cannes and San Remo, where he decides to settle. Publishes *Journal of a Landscape Painter in Corsica*.

1871 Publishes *Nonsense Songs*. Builds a house, the Villa Emily, on the Italian Riviera at San Remo. Acquires his cat Foss.

1872 Publishes *More Nonsense*. Sets out for India, but ill health forces him to turn back at Suez.

1873– Tours India and Ceylon at Northbrook's invitation.
1874

1875 Visits England from June through September.

1877 Publishes *Laughable Lyrics*. Summer in England.

1880 Visits England for the last time, April through August.

1881 Because of a hotel built between Villa Emily and the sea, Lear builds another house, the Villa Tennyson, on another part of the San Remo coast, to be his home until his death. Summers in Monte Generoso, Switzerland, 1881–83, and northern Italy, 1884–87.

1883 Death of Giorgio Kokali.

1885 Carlingford visits San Remo.

1886 Lear suffers a severe case of bronchitis, from which he never fully recovers. Writes his last nonsense poem, "Uncle Arly."

1887 Death of his cat Foss. Gussie, Evelyn Baring, and Lushington visit.

1888 Lear dies at the Villa Tennyson on January 29 and is buried at San Remo.

Chapter One
Life as Nonsense

Writing to his friend Chichester Fortescue in 1873 while in the midst of sorting out three chests of accumulated correspondence and papers, Edward Lear began to ponder his fitness as a biographical subject: "I cannot help thinking that my life, letters and diaries would be as interesting . . . as many that are now published: and I half think I will leave all those papers to you, with a short record of the principal data of my ridiculous life, which however has been a hardworking one, and also one that has given much of various sorts of stuff to others, though the liver has often had a sad time of it."[1] Despite the Victorian vogue for biography and autobiography, no life of Lear appeared until fifty years after his death in 1888, by which time the diaries of his early life and many other letters and papers had been lost.[2] Nevertheless, ample materials remain to document the life that was indeed a hardworking one in which the liver often had a sad time of it. Two full-length biographies, as well as several biographical sketches, now exist, and Lear's story has fascinated many.

Although his extensive travels and acquaintanceship with hundreds of important Victorian aristocrats, government officials, and artists make his biographies and letters an absorbing chronicle of an age, they are read primarily, one suspects, because they serve to decode the autobiography that Lear did after a fashion write: his collected Nonsense. These poems, stories, and drawings do not detail names, places, and dates as do the letters and diaries or the paintings, sketches, and travel journals he issued prodigiously during his lifetime and that constitute the bulk of the "such volumes of stuff" he refers to in his poetic self-portrait "How pleasant to know Mr. Lear!" But the nonsense does provide a faithful record of the emotional ups and downs of Lear's life. In it one finds the loneliness, the instability and lack of certainty about any part of existence, the fear of rejection and abandonment, and the ambivalence about society, marriage, family life, and his own sexuality that made Lear's life so unhappy in the midst of so much genuine love and devotion from his many eminent friends and from generations of children he met on his travels and reached through his books. These books take the form of "nonsense" because the love and the rejection, the patronage by and isolation from society, exist in them side by side, or even defy the laws of physics to occupy the same space. There was a duality, a sense of paradox, involved in almost every aspect of Lear's life, and by abstracting into stylized verse, cartoons, and narrative the conflicting emotions and circumstances that beset him from birth, Lear helped to establish the characteristics of the genre he probably named when he published *A Book of Nonsense* in 1846.

Lear was born May 12, 1812, in a house called Bowman's Lodge in the London suburb of Holloway. He was the twentieth, and youngest to survive infancy, of twenty-one children born to Jeremiah and Ann Clark Skerrett Lear during a twenty-four-year period. Thirteen of the children had died, six in infancy,[3] by the time of his mother's death in 1844, and Lear was to outlive all his siblings, although the ones who reached adulthood proved to be quite longlived. Jeremiah Lear had been in the family sugar refining business, but by the time Edward was born he was working as a stockbroker. In its elegant Georgian house the family lived a prosperous middle-class life with a typical bourgeois retinue of servants and carriages. By 1816, however, Jeremiah Lear had overextended himself, and a series of financial reverses caused him to become a defaulter at the Exchange. He may have spent some time in debtor's prison. The family let Bowman's Lodge and split up, with the older children going out to work and the four-year-old Edward farmed out to the care of his oldest sister Ann, twenty-two years his senior, by his exhausted and harried mother.

Eventually Jeremiah Lear pulled himself out of debt—although the family never again knew affluence—and the Lears moved back into Bowman's Lodge. But Mrs. Lear had abandoned care of Edward for good. Although he lived in the same house with his parents, he was now Ann's charge. Ann, who had a small income left to her by a grandmother, never married and devoted her life to Edward's welfare, fussing over him like the most overprotective of mothers; living with her in his young adulthood, Lear in fact began to feel smothered by her love, although he always regarded her with the greatest affection and gratitude. As Thomas Byrom observes: "He had been an orphan in a family teeming with children; Ann had succeeded in making him at least an only child."[4] Yet this maternal sister could not erase from Lear's memory the fact that his real mother had rejectd him.

Other traumas soon followed this early double catastrophe of sudden poverty and loss of his mother's love. At the age of five Lear experienced his first epileptic seizure. This "Demon," as he called his epilepsy, haunted him for the rest of his life. He marked the frequent occurrence of seizures with heavy black crosses in his diary but hid the nature of his affliction from all his friends and acquaintances. His need to be able to get out of sight when he felt the fit coming on, and the shame that motivated the need, contributed to the isolation he would always feel even among groups of friends and were factors (but hardly the only ones) in preventing him from ever marrying. At seven he suffered from his first prolonged spell of severe depression. And a month before his tenth birthday, a cryptic diary entry of fifty years later seems to indicate, a nineteen-year-old cousin made a homosexual advance toward him. Lear, although probably deceiving himself on this point, believed that the homosexual tendencies he developed as an adult had their origin in this incident. Although one might regard his compulsive traveling as one extended effort to run away from it, Lear never escaped his childhood. Fear of rejection, money worries, epilepsy, depression, and unresolved homosexual longings accompanied him throughout his "life as a wanderer." Perhaps that is why he strove through his nonsense to become the "Old Derry down Derry, who loves to see little folks merry."

If the childhood traumas set the pattern for Lear's life, they also set the pattern for the nonsense. The paradoxes are all there: living in middle-class comfort and yet facing ruin; denied by mother Ann and mothered by sister Ann; sharing physical space with parents yet feeling spiritually parentless. The paradox of happiness subsumed all these. Lear's first period of depression had followed a rare and particularly pleasant excursion with his father, and Lear was always to view happiness as something remembered, lost in the past, but never firmly grasped in the present :"According to the morbid nature of the animal, I even complain sometimes that such rare flashes of light as such visits are to me, make the path darker after they are over . . . I really do believe that I enjoy hardly any one thing on earth while it is present: always looking back, or frettingly peering into the dim beyond."[5]

Lear also must have suffered from the sense of having his destiny predetermined by forces over which he had no control. He could hardly be held responsible for becoming epileptic, prone to depression, homosexual, yet he had to endure the consequences of the catastrophes of his nature as do so many characters in his poetry. There are only a few years during which Lear seems to have controlled his life rather than having been controlled by it— the decade that began with the retirement of his father to Gravesend in 1828, sending Lear and Ann to take rooms off the Gray's Inn Road and Lear at fifteen out to earn a living. It ended with his decision in 1837 to become a traveling landscape painter abroad.

Lear's preparation for a working life came from the dedicated, but amateur, tuition of his sister and from his own reading, observation, and natural talents. His favorite readings included the Romantic poets, particularly Byron, whom he idolized. He may have had a brief period of schooling at age eleven, but his experience with formal education was minimal, a deprivation that did not trouble him much: "I am almost thanking God that I was never educated, for it seems to me that 999 of those who are so, expensively and laboriously, have lost all before they arrive at my age—and remain like Swift's Stulbruggs—cut and dry for life, making no use of their earlier-gained treasures: whereas, I seem to be on the threshold of knowledge, and at least have a long way to the chilling certainty which most men methinks should have, that all labour for light is vain and time thrown away."[6] One part of Ann's teaching, her instructions in drawing and painting in the "painting room" at Bowman's Lodge, brought out an innate ability in young Edward. And when he had to make his way in the world, he chose to do so with pen, pencil, and paint brush.

The subjects he would specialize in drawing and painting seem to have been determined by the same inclinations that attracted him to the Romantics, a love of nature and landscape. This partiality, as well as his desire to become an artist, developed particularly on visits during the years 1823 to 1829 to another of his sisters, Sarah, who had married Charles Street and was living at Arundel in Sussex. Petworth, the estate of the Earl of Egremont, a famous patron of the arts who owned a large collection of paintings, was located twelve miles from Arundel. There Lear met Lord Egremont and other art patrons, viewed the collection, and dreamed of someday emulating Turner.

To prepare to paint landscapes successfully, however, required time and money for lessons, which had to be postponed while Lear sought projects that could bring immediate monetary returns. He began sketching anything that would sell, moved on to "morbid disease drawings, for hospitals and certain doctors of physic," but found his niche as an ornithological and zoological draftsman, illustrating books for various naturalists. Lear soon became so accomplished at this type of art that in 1830, at age eighteen, he commenced work on a fourteen folio (he eventually stopped at twelve) volume of lithographic plates of birds. The result, *Illustrations of the Family of Psittacidae, or Parrots*, published in 1832, established his reputation as an artist of natural history subjects and remains highly regarded. Lear next began working at the London Zoological Gardens on drawings of tortoises and terrapins for a second volume of plates.

While he was making these latter sketches, he was approached by Lord Edward Stanley, heir to the twelfth Earl of Derby, who wanted an artist to draw for publication the animals housed in his large private menagerie at the Derby estate, Knowsley Hall, in Lancashire. Lear's work impressed Stanley, and he invited the young naturalist to undertake the project and live at Knowsley until its completion. Lear eagerly accepted the offer and stayed off and on at Knowsley until 1837.[7] His career as a nonsense artist began at Knowsley also, as his comic rhymes and cartoons endeared him first to the children and then made him an after dinner favorite with the adults, moving him up from the servants' quarters to the main dining room. There he met many members of the British aristocracy and made connections that would gain him introductions wherever in the world English society had established an enclave. He now had hopes of sufficient patronage—four generations of Earls of Derby would be among the most loyal—to realize his dream of traveling abroad and earning a living by painting exotic scenes. His eyesight had never been good, and he could not continue the close work of the natural history drawings without endangering his vision. In addition, the asthma and bronchitis from which he had suffered as a child suddenly became serious threats to his health. So with financial backing from Stanley, now the thirteenth earl, Lear left England in July 1837 for the sunny climate of Rome and life as a landscape painter.

Until this point Lear's history reads like a Victorian novel—deprived childhood, hard work, recognition of his talents, and success. It also has a definite shape and direction. But once he left England his life ceased to follow a straight course and began to move in circles. Reading detailed accounts of Lear's *Wanderjahre* gives one the sense of having landed in the midst of the Caucus Race in the *Alice in Wonderland* of his nonsense contemporary, Lewis Carroll.[8] There were extended stays and repeated visits to the Netherlands, Belgium, Germany, Switzerland,

Italy and Sicily, Malta, the Ionian Islands, Corfu, Greece, Turkey, Albania, Egypt, Palestine, Lebanon, France, India, and Ceylon, and Lear moved around constantly from one place to another within these countries. He also returned to England on twenty different occasions, supervising a gallery in London and making the rounds of the country houses of his friends. All this travel, of course, occurred in the time before airplanes, and Lear was a poor sailor and often in delicate health.

The destinations change, as do the traveling companions, but the pattern of life is the same, unstable and unsettled yet also repetitive and limiting. Lear chose such an existence and then, partly because of external factors and partly because of his own nature, became incapable of choosing another. The paradox of unpredictability joined with monotony that characterized this way of life dictated the world view one finds in his nonsense. How that double-edged universe evolved becomes apparent upon examination of the dualities Lear experienced for the last fifty years of his life concerning the most fundamental human needs: to have a home, to earn a living, and to find love and companionship.

It is difficult to decide whether a cruel fate decreed that the sense of homelessness Lear must have felt as a four-year-old displaced from Bowman's Lodge and his mother's affections should never leave him, or whether, always fearful of losing a permanent home, Lear avoided all opportunities to establish one. Probably both elements contributed to his nomadic life. Fate certainly had determined that he could never settle permanently in England. His respiratory ailments would not allow him to weather the damp, cold English winters. His one attempt to make England his home base for an extended period lasted from July 1849 to December 1853, when he was participating in the ten-year course in painting offered by the Royal Academy Schools. But the climate took its toll, and he realized that he could never last out the decade in England; as he wrote Emily Tennyson in October 1853:

I am turning over in every way some mode of leaving this loathsome climate & getting a living for the remainder of my life, even if as a shoeblack, so I could see the sun. Perhaps I may go & fight the Russians—perhaps go to Australia. But stay here I won't, to be demoralized by years of mud & fog & gnats and rheumatism & small beer and stupid bores and coalfires and choleramorbusses and income taxes and calvinists and steel forks and humbugs and midnight atmospheres all the year round.[9]

In December he gave up his ambition of completing the course and sailed for the Near East.

Ironically, the sunny climes to which Lear fled to avoid English winters generally proved too hot and fever-producing in the summers, so that he would have to pull up stakes once again, often to return to England to exhibit his works in a set of rooms he rented in Stratford Place. Seasonal migration became part of the cycle of his life:

> And thence I only come again
> Just to pack up and run
> Somewhere where life may less be pain,
> And somewhere where there's sun.[10]

When, in his last years, he became too frail to make the journey to England, he traveled to Monte Generoso in Switzerland, and finally to the mountains of northern Italy.

In his search for a winter base of operations to fit into this monotonous pattern, Lear encountered the capriciousness of existence that always accompanied the monotony in his life. Lear established himself in Rome from 1838 to 1848, but he left to take up the Royal Academy course. When he returned there in 1858, he was only able to remain for two years before the political turmoil in Italy made the prospect of English visitors, and therefore customers for his paintings, uncertain. "If you are absolutely alone in the world, & likely to be so," he wrote Fortescue at this time, "then move about continually & never stand still. I therefore think I shall be compulsed & more especially by the appearance of things on the horizon,—to go to Japan & New York, or Paraguay, or anywhere before long."[11]

One of his favorite places was Corfu, where he had lived from 1855 to 1858 and from 1862 to 1863. However, when he returned to the island once more in January 1864, perhaps with an eye toward settling there, he discovered that with the accession of Prince William of Denmark to the Greek throne the preceding summer, Corfu was to be abandoned by the British garrison there and restored to Greek authority. So, having barely unpacked, Lear would once again have to think of somewhere else to go: "By April or May at furthest, I shall hope to be fixed as to fixing or unfixing: perhaps I may go about in an unfixed mode continually and evermore. What's the odds?"[12]

Lear finally did "fix" himself in 1871 when he purchased some land and built a house, the Villa Emily, on the Mediterranean at San Remo in northwestern Italy. And here one last time fate pulled the rug out from under him. In 1879, despite promises to the contrary, the owners of a strip of land between the villa and the sea permitted some German land developers to construct a tall hotel there. The hotel would cater primarily to the "Germen, Gerwomen, and Gerchildren" whom Lear for "some irrational reason," as Lady Strachey puts it, detested. Furthermore, the structure blocked his view of the sea, and reflections from its white wall ruined the light in his studio. Lear was thrown into despair, and only a kind loan from several of his friends, which enabled him to build a new house on another part of the San Remo coast, allowed him to have a secure home for the last eight years of his life. "What's the odds?" Lear must have felt them to be stacked firmly against him.

Nevertheless, Lear was the one who had chosen a career that would necessitate a great deal of travel; when any of his friends suggested a trip to some far-off locale, he always eagerly consented to go. Even had circumstances not gone against him, there was a restlessness in Lear's nature that would not permit him to settle, at least not until his old age when failing health made travel really arduous. Another remark in a letter to Fortescue is pertinent: "How I wish I had some settled abode, at least until the last narrow box. But if I settled myself I should go to Tobago the next day." His travels often became a means of running away from misfortune, but he could not escape the sadness within. The deep unhappiness that had settled in Lear's heart during his child-hood, one suspects, pushed him on. It is probably most accurate to say that Lear initially chose to live as a wanderer, and by the time he decided that he might want to live otherwise, he had lost the ability to change his destiny.[13] His desires and the limitations of his nature coincided at first, then turned on each other to trap him, a dilemma that would become all too familiar to the characters in his nonsense works.

Lear's chosen profession as a landscape painter, besides con-tributing to his unsettled state, entailed additional paradoxes. The saddest involved the fact that of all Lear's varied artistic en-deavors—natural-history draftsmanship, topographical sketching, watercolors, nonsense cartooning—the large landscape oil paintings upon which he hoped to base his reputation and accordingly sell for considerable sums were the only artistic productions with which he failed. When accepted at Royal Academy exhibitions, they were generally displayed badly and not favorably reviewed. While Lear's large pool of patrons guaranteed eventual sale, and he painted other oils on commission, no general demand for Lear landscapes akin to that for Turners or Constables ever developed. The history of his large picture *The Cedars of Lebanon* illustrates his difficulties as a landscape painter.

He began work on this nine-foot-long canvas in 1860, an am-bitious project he undertook in order not to "turn into a stagnant snail."[14] Lear completed it in May 1861, two months after the death of his sister Ann, for whose last days he had fortuitously been in England and not, as Ann gratefully noted, "among the Arabs." He decided to price *The Cedars* at 700 guineas and ex-hibited it in a Liverpool gallery where it garnered glowing com-ments from a local critic but attracted no buyers. In April 1862 he entered it in the Great International Exhibition in London.

But there it hung high, and Tom Taylor gave it an unfavorable notice in the *Times*. Lear could not sell the painting until December 1867 and then for only 200 pounds. But by this time, six and a half years after its completion, he was glad to sell it for any price, his despair about the fate of *The Cedars* having caused him on various occasions to muse humorously about turning it into a carpet or a cloak.

Large oil paintings simply were not Lear's forte. His watercolor sketches increase yearly in value and in the esteem with which modern art critics regard them.[15] But, as Vivien Noakes remarks: "He never fully understood what he was doing when he painted in oils, and in his anxiety he often overworked the pictures until all the sparkle had gone and the fluid, rhythmical movement which made his water colours so delightful had been ground to a standstill."[16] Yet Lear believed to the end that the oil paintings represented his true art and considered the watercolors as mere jobbery, turned out to keep him supplied with "reddy tin."

Nothing illustrates his attitude so pointedly as the system he worked out in the 1860s to increase his productivity in turning out sketches for sale. It was a kind of assembly-line concept designed to produce in the most efficient manner a large number of salable pictures. Lear called the results of this system his "tyrants." For the first group of sixty tyrants, which he began in December 1863, Lear chose sixty rough sketches, mounted sixty canvases—thirty large and thirty small ones—drew outlines on each one, then painted the blues on each, next the greens, the browns, and so forth. In sixty days he had completed the sixty watercolors. The following year he produced 240 tyrants in batches of eighty at a time. Besides demonstrating the cavalier attitude that Lear took toward the art at which he most excelled, this pragmatic and rather appalling systemization of creativity symbolically expresses another of the paradoxes of his life. By choosing a career as an artist, Lear would seem to have guaranteed himself a certain amount of freedom and flexibility in earning a living. And yet he was cranking out paintings with as much monotonous routine as a worker in one of the factories of Victorian industrial England.

The tiresome rounds of exhibiting his works in portions of his various lodgings set aside as galleries followed. Moreover, the monotony of producing the paintings was not at least compensated for by a steady income. Sales always came irregularly and payment after sales more irregularly still. Although Lear never lived in actual poverty, and could always count on loans from his friends,[17] he never knew with certainty from month to month how much money would be coming in, and he often endured considerably straitened circumstances. Therefore, entrapment in dull routine intermingled with instability of fortunes in yet another area of Lear's endeavors.

Lear frequently commented ruefully on the contradictions his wandering life and artistic occupation entailed, but the difficulties these brought on were of minor importance in comparison to the central paradox of his emotional life that had begun with his infant isolation within a large family: a persistent loneliness, even when surrounded by large number of persons. From Turin in 1870 he wrote Fortescue: "I live the queerest solitary life here, in company of seventy people."[18] In fact, crowds increased his sense of isolation. He felt less despondent when alone than when crowded. He said that he would only consent to go to heaven if St. Peter promised him no more than ten persons around him at a time; and he would desire the angels to keep their distance. Even during the exciting early plays at Knowsley "Lear sometimes felt horribly lonely, and then he would escape from all the busy guests and walk alone through the park."[19] Lear constantly moved in the higher echelons of British society—he had given drawing lessons to Queen Victoria in 1846, and members of the Royal family occasionally purchased works and visited his studio when they were on junkets abroad—but although most of his close friends came from its ranks, he disliked "Society" as an entity. He found too many fashionable Englishmen abroad narrow-minded, dull, and snobbish. And yet these people bought his paintings, provided his livelihood. The opportunity to associate with such company would not ordinarily have opened to a man of Lear's background, but with the extension of his social horizons came a dependency on people he would not have chosen to depend upon, a paradox of freedom and limitation once more.

Lear was by temperament, however, quite the opposite from a loner. He overflowed with affection, a childish desire to please that served to endear him in turn to the children for whom he initially produced his nonsenses. It also gained him the loyal friends with whom he corresponded and traveled and who helped him through financial difficulties, opened their homes to him when he was in England, and listened sympathetically as he poured out his unhappiness. Lear considered friendship a serious affair with inherent duties not to be taken lightly. This was one reason why he felt so lonely among the transient populations at the European watering holes, no matter how cordially they might receive him. From his villa at San Remo he remarks in the winter of 1875, "No creature here is likely to interest me this year. At 63— (and speaking as a man who never cared for mere acquaintances), one hardly picks up friends."[20]

He constantly marveled that he had acquired and kept such a large number of friends, but he probably did so by acting as such a splendid friend himself. Among the many friends who figured prominently in Lear's life were Bernard Husey Hunt (*né* Senior) from Sussex; Robert Hornby from the Knowsley days; Chichester Fortescue, later Lord Carlingford; Franklin Lushington; Alfred and, especially, Emily Tennyson; the cousins Thomas and Evelyn Baring, later Lords Northbrook and Cromer; William Holman Hunt; and Hubert Congreve, son of Lear's neighbor at San Remo, Walter Congreve.

In some respects, however, barriers separated Lear from even these close friends. Three peers and the Poet Laureate who was to become one, an influential judge (Lushington), one of the leaders of the Pre-Raphaelite Brotherhood,[21] simply moved in different circles than a virtually classless "dirty landscape painter,"[22] and had their time differently occupied. Fortescue, Lushington, and Thomas Baring were involved in government duties and colonial administration that made their paths sometimes cross Lear's abroad, but they and most of his other friends had solid establishments in England where Lear was only a visitor, and one who had a knack for dropping in at the worst possible times. His health and occupation had doomed him to settle far from those he cared about most. And as his friends married one by one he felt further estranged from them. His friendships flourished through the post, but their face to face manifestations were irregular and not totally satisfactory.

Lear's only regular companions for any length of time were his Suliot manservant Giorgio Kokali, often anglicized as "George" in Lear's letters and diaries, who served Lear for twenty-seven years, and Lear's cat Foss, celebrated in many drawings, whom he owned for seventeen years. But national differences, a family in Corfu, and his status as servant distanced Giorgio from his employer; and Foss, after all, was only a cat. Both predeceased Lear, as had so many of his acquaintances and all the members of his large family. Although several friends made extended visits to the Villa Tennyson during Lear's final illness, when he died on January 29, 1888, he was alone except for a servant. He had addressed his last words to all those absent friends:

My good Giuseppe, I feel that I am dying. You will render me a sacred service in telling my friends and relations that my last thought was for them, especially the Judge and Lord Northbrook and Lord Carlingford. I cannot find words sufficient to thank my good friends for the good they have always done me. I did not answer their letters because I could not write, as no sooner did I take a pen in my hand than I felt as if I were dying.[23]

After attending the funeral, Madam Philipp, then the wife of Lear's physician, Dr. Hassall, expressed for one last time the paradox involved in Lear's many friendships: "I have never forgotten it, it was all so sad, so lonely. After such a life as Mr Lear's had been and the immense number of friends he had, there was not one of them able to be with him at the end."[24]

Regarding relationships more intimate than friendship, Lear experienced even more heartache. While no documented evidence demonstrates that Lear ever engaged in homosexual practices, all his passionate attachments certainly involved men, not women. The most intense of these focused on Franklin Lushington, whom Lear had met in Malta and had traveled with throughout Greece for six blissful weeks in the spring of 1849 when Lushington was twenty-seven. During this journey Lushington proved an exuberant and totally compatible companion, and Lear had fallen deeply in love with him by the time it had ended. For Lushington, however, the journey had apparently served as one final, uninhibited holiday before he assumed the graver responsibilities of adulthood. At their next meeting Lear found him cold and distant. Although their friendship continued till the end of Lear's life—he made Lushington his executor—Lushington's inability (or unwillingness) to return even a fraction of the older man's passion tormented Lear to the point of madness.

Later in his life Lear was strongly attracted to young Hubert Congreve, who lived at San Remo. Lear, forty years Hubert's senior, had met him in 1869 and tutored him in drawing from his boyhood. He dreamed that Hubert would one day come to live with him at the Villa Tennyson and seriously study painting. Hubert dashed Lear's hopes when he chose to return to England and matriculate at King's College in 1877. They continued to meet and travel together after Hubert left San Remo, but Lear's longings for permanent companionship had been denied once more; in the summer of Hubert's departure he came very close to a nervous breakdown, as he also had when his relationship with Lushington was at its most strained. In 1910, writing the preface to the second volume of Lear's letters to Fortescue, Hubert recalled him as "a man of versatile and original genious [*sic*], with great gifts, one of the most interesting, affectionate, and lovable characters it has been my good fortune to know and to love."[25] He doubtless never realized that the kind of love he gave Lear could never satisfy his friend's deeper need. Lear tragically fixed his affections again and again on those who could not reciprocate. He appears to have had little interest in homosexual acquaintances such as John Addington Symonds.

His homosexuality must have contributed to Lear's reluctance to marry. When he theorizes about marriage in his letters, he generally instances a time when he is old, feeble, and in need of care as the proper moment for him to take a wife. Marriage might fulfill his need for companionship, for someone with whom to share his problems, but he never seems to have deceived himself into thinking he could feel sexual desire for a woman. When thinking of a wife, he was really thinking of someone to replace Ann and the mother who had given him up. But his nomadic way of life, his precarious financial situation, the impossibility of hiding his epilepsy from a spouse, the fear that a woman would again reject him made even marriage on these terms appear a risky proposition. Lear also believed that his large nose, long legs, and weak eyesight made him too ugly to attract women, although his photographs reveal, while definitely not a handsome, certainly a quite pleasant-looking man.

Nevertheless, Lear never stopped toying with the idea of marrying, and in two instances went so far as having a definite prospect in mind. Lear met the first prospect, Helena Cortazzi, on Corfu in 1856. She was the daughter of an Italian father and an English mother, who was a relation of Lear's friends from Lancashire, the Hornbys. Lear admired her grace and her enthusiasm for poetry and art, and he wrote to his friends about his susceptibility to her charms. However, their mutual lack of money and the fact that one could not "unmarry again if it didn't suit!" kept him from committing himself to any serious relationship. In 1858, when Lear was spending a miserable winter on Corfu, from which the Cortazzis had departed the previous summer, he declared that "If Helena Cortazzi had been here, it would have been useless to think of avoiding asking her to marry me, even had I never so little trust in the wisdom of such a step."[26] But, of course, she was not there. And as Vivien Noakes remarks, "if she had been there he wouldn't have done so. The few amorous sentiments Lear expressed towards unattached women faded when he was actually with them and they were no longer safely unattainable."[27]

Lear's most serious relationship with a woman, one that came to the brink of a proposal of marriage, involved Augusta Bethell, daugther of Richard Bethell, Lord Westbury. Lear had known "Gussie" from her childhood, but after a visit to the Westbury home in November 1862, when she was twenty-four, he began to consider her as a possible mate. He characteristically vacillated for five years, but in October 1867 he went up to the Westburys' with the idea of proposing to Gussie. Unfortunately, he first consulted her sister Emma about the advisability of such a move. Emma, probably for reasons of class and money, strongly disapproved and convinced Lear that the marriage would be impossible. He left without approaching Gussie—who doubtless would have given him a very different answer. In 1872 she married a man named Adamson Parker, many years her senior, an almost total invalid, not wealthy, and, as Lear wrote to Fortescue, "one who is disapproved of as her husband by all the family."[28] Her choice seems almost symbolic, as if she had gone out of her way (and perhaps she had) to select a man who possessed exaggerated versions of all those faults that Lear thought stood in the way of their union. Given the nature of Lear's experience, such a turn of events was almost to be expected. After Parker died in 1882, Gussie visited Lear several times in San Remo and nursed him during his last illness. Once again, in his seventies and ill, Lear pondered a proposal; but he died without making one.

Lear had only one really satisfactory relationship with a woman, Emily Tennyson, whom he met in 1849 when she was already married to the poet and therefore could serve as a confidante and comforter to Lear without threatening him as a potential matrimonial prospect. She replaced Ann as mother-figure in the sophisticated aristocratic and artistic world that Lear traveled in but that was completely beyond the experience of his devoted sister. Although Lear and Alfred Tennyson did not enjoy a very warm personal relationship,[29] he kept up their acquaintance and visited them frequently in order to stay close to the Emily he idolized:

I should think computing moderately, that 15 angels, several hundreds of ordinary women, many philosophers, a heap of truly wise and kind mothers, 3 or 4 minor prophets, and a lot of doctors and school-mistresses, might all be boiled down, and yet their combined essence fall short of what Emily Tennyson really is.[30]

Few people or events in Lear's life presented such a harmonious combination of elements as he saw in Emily. His existence, as we have seen, overflowed with contradictions that resolutely refused to come together. Lear's reactions to this paradoxical existence display as many ups and downs as did his life. Sometimes he accepts the vagaries of life philosophically: "Things must be as they may, and the best is to make the best of what happens." Sometimes they force him to cry out in anger: "There are times when I turn into bile and blackness, body & soul,—& in those phases of life I hate myself & through myself hate everybody, even those I like best." And sometimes he stands paralyzed with indecision: "Woke to impatience, blindness and misery, incapable of deciding whether life can be cured or cursed. I totter giddily, refusing to take any road, yet agonized by staying irresolute." In general, however, his experiences taught him never to be surprised at anything with which life confronted him. He also learned that in a world so complex and many-sided any kind of narrow exclusiveness was folly. In life and art he both expressed and embraced all facets of existence. Of the many demonstrations of this attitude, one may by way of example point to the variety of his artistic techniques and to his attitude toward religion.

Works from the different categories of Lear's efforts as draftsman and painter vary so thoroughly in style and point of view that one hardly recognizes them as coming from the same artist. The natural history drawings are minutely detailed and, to use a cinematic metaphor, in close-up. His topographical water color sketches and oil landscape paintings had by their nature to be in extreme long shot; many display a certain vagueness of detail, and they reduce any people they contain to small, indistinct figures in the foreground. Lear never mastered the art of realistic figure drawing, and the only works to deal repeatedly with human beings are the medium range views in the stylized cartoon caricatures— including many self-caricatures—that make up the bulk of the nonsense drawings. Together these varied types of art comprise a comprehensive view of life impossible with any one style.

In religion, Lear rejected narrowness of focus just as he did in art. He considered himself a Christian, but the activities of organized Christianity in the nineteenth century disgusted him. After several abortive attempts to reach both, he made pilgrimages to Mount Athos (1856) and Jerusalem (1858), only to be appalled at what he saw when he arrived. In one of the most widely quoted passages from his letters he castigates the monastic seclusion of Mount Athos:

> The name of Christ on every garment and at every tongue's end, but his maxims trodden under foot. God's world and will turned upside down, maimed, & caricatured:—if this I say be Xtianity let Xtianity be rooted out as soon as possible. More pleasing in the sight of the Almighty I really believe, & more like what Jesus Christ intended man to become, is an honest Turk with 6 wives, or a Jew working hard to feed his little old clo' babbies, than these muttering, miserable, mutton-hating, man-advoiding, misogynic, morose, & merriment-marring, monotoning, many-mule-making, mocking, mournful, minced-fish & marmalade masticating Monx.[31]

The bickering of various factions of the Christian community in Jerusalem likewise dismayed him. As he did in his comments on the Athos monks, he expressed a preference for non-Christian religions over the type of Christianity he had encountered: "By Heaven! if I wished to prevent a Turk, Hebrew, or Heathen, from turning Christian I would send him straight to Jerusalem! I vow I could have turned Jew myself, as one American has actually lately done."[32] He could never accept the Athanasian Creed because of its "hateful exclusion principle." He sided with Bishop Colenso and the authors of "Essays and Reviews." He despised provincial religious zeal, even in his brothers and sisters who had emigrated to New Zealand and America. He felt that true Christianity had an inverse relation to orthodoxy; had he his own chapel, he said, "Belfast Protestantism, Athanasian creeds, and all kinds of moony miracles should have no entrance there: but a plain worship of God, and a perpetual endeavour at progress." And he thought that most of the fashionable clergymen who preached to the English congregations abroad were unthinking "asses." They had such assurance in their narrow dogma, and Lear knew first hand that one could never be sure of anything.

This world view, engendered by his experiences, is best expressed, however, in nonsense writing, the activity that produced still another paradox of Lear's life and reputation. Although Lear, ever industrious and ever aware of possibilities for increasing the supply of tin through his exertions, did not neglect the opportunity to collect his nonsenses, prepare them for publication, and urge friends to recommend them to others, as he did similarly with his travel journals, he did not write nonsenses in order to make a living. Drawing and painting were his full-time occupations; he produced nonsense as a means of special communication with friends, both children and adults. Nonsense came to him spontaneously, without being worked at as his pictures were. As he phrased it in 1863, "Nonsense issues from me at times—to make a new book next year."[33] While hoping to make hundreds of guineas on his larger paintings, Lear felt supremely lucky to receive £125 for the copyright to the *Book of Nonsense*.

Nevertheless his friends felt that "in his heart of hearts" he was fonder of his nonsense books than of his paintings. Hubert Congreve notes that unfavorable or ill-informed reviews of the nonsense books disturbed Lear, "yet criticisms of his pictures he always took unconcernedly, and would frequently laugh over them." Certainly favorable comments on the nonsense delighted him, in particular Ruskin's remark in the *Pall Mall Magazine* in February 1886 that "I don't know of any author to whom I am half so grateful for my idle self as Edward Lear. I shall put him first of my hundred authors." Lear was also pleased, and somewhat astonished, to hear allusions to the *Book of Nonsense* in Parliamentary debate and to have selections from his books quoted back to him by children and adults in far corners of the globe. After fifty years of exhausting labor to establish himself as a landscape painter, Lear ended his career barely recognized as an artist but renowned for his avocation as "the Author of the Book of Nonsense"—the final vagary of fate, or as Lear phrased it "sich is phame."

Thus, because of the way in which the events of his life had unfolded, Lear could hardly have avoided succeeding as a nonsense poet. A favorite anecdote of his involved overhearing a conversation about the *Book of Nonsense* and its author among a gentleman and some ladies traveling with him in a train compartment in England. All acknowledged the delightful nature of the nonsense and praised its creator, Edward Lear. The gentleman then announced knowingly that "Edward Lear" was a fiction, his name an anagram of "Edward, Earl," which thus identified the true author as the Earl of Derby (to whom Lear had dedicated the book). Several reviews had made a similar claim, the reasons for which confusion Lear now understood. The poet hastened to correct the gentleman: "That is quite a mistake: I have reason to know that Edward Lear the painter and author wrote and illustrated the whole book." Rather than admit his error, the gentleman challenged Lear's assertion: "And I . . . have good reason to know, Sir, that you are wholly mistaken. *There is no such a person* as Edward Lear." Lear then triumphantly informed him: "But . . . there *is*—and I am the man—and I wrote the book!" None of the listeners, however, believed him, and he had to produce the name and address label on the inside of his hat, a monogrammed handkerchief, and his card to establish his identity, at which point, finally, "amazement devoured those benighted individuals and I left them to gnash their teeth in trouble and tumult."[34]

The joke should have been on the pompous gentleman, brought low in an archetypal comic conflict between *alazon* and *eiron*. And yet how mortifying, and in a Kafkaesque way how frightening, for Lear in 1866 at the height of his career to encounter a man who not only had never heard of him but who denied his very existence. In even the most secure aspect of Lear's life, his knowledge of his own identity, suddenly certainty evaporates.

Lear illustrated this encounter with a drawing of himself in a realistic style (one of the few of his self-portraits that is not a caricature) facing the gentleman, who resembles one of the characters in Lear's limericks. Sense squares off with nonsense, right on

Lear confronts the man on the train.

an ordinary English train; Lear ponders an image of the pattern of his life. The drawing and the incident, which one suspects Lear may have embroidered upon in the telling, emblemize the double-sidedness, the coexisting contradictoriness that will occur again and again in the nonsense literature with which the rest of this study will deal. They also once again express the paradox of security and freedom that will form a major theme of the nonsense, as Lear, secure in his superior position to the gentleman, has to scramble to establish his identity while, conversely, the unrestrained and uninformed speech of the gentleman must finally be constrained to embarrassed silence and gnashing of teeth.

Lear did not create a nonsense world in his imagination but

found it in his day-to-day experiences. He expressed his feelings about such a world in a poetic fragment, unpublished at his death, which Angus Davidson calls "a perfectly *serious* poem in the Lear manner" and "one of the purest pieces of nonsense he ever wrote":

> Cold are the crabs that crawl on yonder hills,
> Colder the cucumbers that grow beneath,
> And colder still the brazen chops that wreathe
>   The tedious gloom of philosophic pills!
> For when the tardy gloom of nectar fills
> The ample bowls of demons and of men,
> There lurks the feeble mouse, the homely hen,
>   And there the porcupine with all her quills.
> Yet much remains—to weave a solemn strain
> That lingering sadly—slowly dies away,
> Daily departing with departing day.
> A pea green gamut on a distant plain
> When wily walrusses in congress meet—
>   Such such is life—[35]

Such *is* life, for life to Lear was nonsense.

Chapter Two
The Limericks

Structural Patterns

Lear began composing comic rhymes with accompanying fanciful drawings for the amusement of the children, and later the entire household, at Knowsley from 1832 to 1836. He found an appealing formula to contain his fancies when he came across an illustrated volume of humor, published in 1822 or thereabouts, entitled *Anecdotes and Adventures of Fifteen Gentlemen*. One humorous verse read:

> There was a sick man of Tobago
> Liv'd long on rice-gruel and sago;
> But at last, to his bliss,
> The physician said this—
> 'To a roast leg of mutton you may go.'

This type of verse, whose precise origins are uncertain, came to be known, again for uncertain reasons, as a limerick.

It is certain that Lear, although hardly the originator of the limerick form, was the first poet to gain fame as a writer of limericks, and his works expanded the popularity of the form enormously. His first volume of verse, *A Book of Nonsense,* published pseudononymously in 1846, collects a decade and a half of limericks and contains no poetry of any other kind. When Lear revised and enlarged this volume for a new edition in 1861 under his own name, it still included none of his longer poems, with which he only began experimenting during the succeeding decade. The first manuscript of a nonsense song that Lear circulated is that of "The Owl and the Pussy—cat," which he presented to Janet

24

Symonds in December 1867. Even after venturing upon more ambitious nonsense, he continued to produce limericks and included one hundred new ones in his third book of verse, *More Nonsense Pictures, Rhymes, Botany &c* (1872). For thirty years as a self-proclaimed nonsense poet, Lear considered nonsense synonymous with limericks. Since the many versifiers who have followed Lear into the limerick field produce light verse or ribald verse, but rarely nonsense verse, one point that a consideration of the limericks should bring out is the precise qualities that make them nonsense. Before one jumps to any hasty conclusions, a survey of the structure and subject matter of the limericks is in order.

The following verse represents the limerick form that Lear most often employs, the archetypal Learian limerick, as it were:

> There was an old person of Deal
> Who in walking, used only his heel;
> When they said, 'Tell us why?'—He made no reply;
> That mysterious old person of Deal.[1]

All of Lear's limericks begin "There was . . ."[2] and go on to announce the existence of an individual who is in the literal sense remarkable, i.e. something about his or her appearance, behavior, or circumstances is worthy of remark. Most of the limerick protagonists are extremely singular, going far beyond the pale of that sick man of Tobago who simply had to restrict his diet until his doctor said otherwise. They engage in eccentric and often impossible behavior; their heads are too small, their noses and legs too long, their eating habits and ideas of fashion strange. They fall victim to terrible calamities. They come into conflict with neighbors, the infamous "they" of Lear's world, and with the animal kingdom, but they also on occasion develop satisfying symbiotic relationships with both. The emotions of some tend toward extremes—despair, frenzy, fury, elation—but others are infuriatingly inscrutable, reacting calmly to the most trying situations. needed in order to establish their identities. The generic desig-

These limerick protagonists may be identified as either an Old Man, Old or Young Person (who may be either male or female) and Old or Young Lady. Lear interestingly never dubs any of the characters a Young Man. But even Young Ladies and Persons appear rarely. The Young Lady occurs in twenty-one of the 112 limericks in the *Book of Nonsense* but in only seven of the one hundred "Nonsense Rhymes and Pictures" in *More Nonsense*,[3] the Young Person in a mere ten in all. The Old Lady appears in only five. So by far the majority of limerick protagonists—169 of 212—are either Old Men or Persons. Their relative proportions shift from the earlier to the later nonsense. The *Book of Nonsense* contains fifty-six Old Men and twenty-nine Old Persons, while *More Nonsense* contains thirty-three Old Men and fifty-one Old Persons. Coupled with the reduction of the number of Young Ladies in *More Nonsense,* this change to the neutral designation leads to the conclusion that Lear began to think of his individuals more as similar to each other, in contrast with the people around them, than according to the differences in sex or age among them. As Lear was reporting completion of *More Nonsense* to Fortescue in July 1870, he described the volume as containing "9 songs—110 'old persons' and other rubbish and fun." Lear probably also preferred to employ "old" characters in order to delight his nursery audience with the antics of bizarre adults at a time when so much children's literature attempted to teach moral lessons about the misbehavior of young people.

The generic designations given the men, ladies, and persons, often linked to their places of origin, constitute their sole appellations; no limerick protagonist bears a proper name, although we occasionally learn the name of one of his relatives, e.g. Opsibeena, daughter of the Old Man of Messina, or Euphemia, daughter of the Old Man of Bohemia. The anonymity derives from the older limericks that were Lear's source, and "There was a young lady from . . ." has remained a popular limerick opening. However, the formula additionally suits the content of Lear's limericks well. His characters are so very remarkable that a proper name is hardly nation also serves as a distancing device, making readers more likely to accept without question the odd goings-on in the verses.

The sick man came from Tobago, and the majority of the limerick protagonists are also linked to a specific locality, many of which the peripatetic Lear had visited during his travels. In the first series of limericks, however, a rather sizable minority—forty of the 112—do not name the protagonist's place of origin. But Lear obviously grew fonder of the geographical associations, since the number of characters whose homes are not specified declines to eighteen in the second series. The use of these real place names contributes to the overall nonsensicalness of the limericks by creating a tension between the actual and the impossible. Many events in the poems could not occur outside the boundaries of fantasy, but instead of situating the action in a make-believe world (as he will do in some of the longer poems), Lear sets them in known, if sometimes exotic, places. As will become clear subsequently, this tension is only one of many that inform the limericks and express in them the prevailing Learian paradox.

Once Lear has established the identity of his protagonist, he goes on in a relative clause to report the action, characteristics, situation, or interaction with others that make the individual remarkable. If the protagonist is "of" somewhere, the relative clause begins in the second line. If not, the relative pronoun may occur in the second half of line one to accommodate a longer clause ("There was a Young Lady whose bonnet,/Came untied when the birds sate upon it"), although sometimes another prepositional phrase substitutes for "of [locality]": "There was an Old Man with a nose." Only nine limericks—usually rather awkward in construction—do not contain relative clauses in the second line and many of these merely use appositives instead:

> There was an Old Man of Leghorn
> The smallest as ever was born;
> But quickly snapt up he, was once by a puppy,
> Who devoured that Old Man of Leghorn.[4]

The third line (or third and fourth, depending upon the way in which the limerick is reproduced typographically) displays the most versatility, falling into no predominant pattern, although "he (she) said" or "they said" often figures in somewhere. This section of the limerick details the consequences of the state of affairs described in the first two lines. This description may carry over to the final line,[5] but a substantial number of times—ninety of 212—the limerick concludes with an exclamation about the protagonist: "That [adjective] Old Person of [locality]." The adjective sometimes is justified by what has gone before:

> There was an Old Person of Gretna,
> Who rushed down the crater of Etna;
> When they said, 'Is it hot?' He replied, 'No, it's not!'
> That mendacious Old Person of Gretna.[6]

But at other times no logical connection between this judgment and the character's behavior is apparent:

> There was an old person of Rye,
> Who went up to town on a fly;
> But they said, 'If you cough, you are safe to fall off!
> You abstemious old Person of Rye!'[7]

Whether or not it conforms to the syntactical pattern just discussed, the last line almost invariably ends with the same word as the first. Only fourteen verses stray from this model, several of these repeating the final word of the second line in the last. It is quite rare for the three A-rhymes of the a a b b a rhyme scheme to comprise three different words as in

> There was an Old Lady whose folly,
> Induced her to sit in a holly;
> Whereon by a thorn, her dress being torn,
> She quickly became melancholy.[8]

The refrain effect from which the last example departs distinguishes Lear's limericks from those that have subsequently evolved, for later limerick writers generally aim at a clever twist for the last rhyme to serve as a kind of punch line. Lear's method makes the verse more closed and balanced and, some might argue, more monotonous. But the inevitability of Lear's final rhymes fittingly complements the whole tendency of his versification in these poems.

I have enumerated the various structural patterns of the limericks in such wearisome detail in order to stress the thoroughness with which Lear strives to make an already strictly defined and limited verse form more rigid still. (The number of departures from the typical patterns decreases noticeably in the later series.) And he does this, it appears, to create another of those paradoxes that make his poems nonsense rather than mere light verse. For if the verse form becomes confining and conventionalized, the people and events portrayed therein repeatedly stray from the norms of everyday life. As they are trapped in the poetic structure, so most of the limerick protagonists struggle to alter some confining aspects of their existence. And Lear, in keeping with the duality that marks his life and works, views their rebellion as sometimes commendable and heroic, sometimes ill-advised, silly, and even dangerous.

"They" and the others

The most celebrated theme of the limericks involves the relationship between the eccentric individual and the society around him, the depersonalized "people of," more often simply "they." Although "they" appear in a little under half of the poems, their treatment of the protagonist has caught the imagination of most Lear critics. Angus Davidson comments: "What a world of implication there is in Lears 'they!' 'They' are the force of public opinion, the dreary voice of human mediocrity: 'they' are perpetually interfering with the liberty of the individual: 'they' gossip, 'they' condemn, 'they' are inquisitive and conventional and almost always uncharitable."[9] George Orwell cites the fate of the Old Man of Whitehaven, "smashed" for dancing a quadrille with a raven: "To smash somebody just for dancing a quadrille with a raven is exactly the kind of thing that 'They' would do."[10] Orwell might also have mentioned the Old Man with a gong, similarly smashed for being "a horrid old bore," or the half dozen other verses in which "they" inflict physical harm on the otherwise unquenchable nonconformist.

Yet by focusing on these particular limericks, the critics have oversimplified the situation, making one-sided a conflict that, like most things in Lear, is double-edged.[11] The relationship between the individual and "them" has several facets. One can roughly classify the forms the relationship takes as follows:

1. "They" are hostile and quell the innocent individual.
2. "They" are hostile, but the individual quells them.
3. "They" are hostile, but the individual is culpable in provoking their anger.
4. "They" express a netural interest which the individual rebuffs.
5. The manner in which the individual expresses his individuality pleases "them", and "they" extend approval.
6. The individual is in difficulty, and "they" try to help him, or vice versa.

To be sure, some verses fall ambiguously into seemingly exclusive categories—this is nonsense, after all. The help "they" offer the Old Man of the Dee to rid himself of a troublesome flea is rather sinister: "When he said, 'I will scratch it'—they gave him a hatchet,/Which grieved that Old Man of the Dee."[12] "They" do help the Old Man of Aôsta finds his missing cow but get in some of their frequent taunts in the process: "But they said, 'Don't you see, she has rushed up a tree?/You invidious Old Man of Aôsta!' "[13]

It is therefore understandable that readers of the limericks should neglect the more benign interactions between the individual and "them," for "their" antagonism appears far more regularly, and even "their" aid may turn deadly. Although actual physical attacks do not occur in most instances, "they" often attack the protagonist verbally, criticizing his personal appearance and habits, taunting him with questions, and generally making him feel a misfit:

> There was an Old Man of Melrose,
> Who walked on the tips of his toes;
> But they said, 'It ain't pleasant, to see you at present,
> You stupid Old Man of Melrose.'[14]

> There was an old man of Dumblane,
> Who greatly resembled a crane;
> But they said,—'Is it wrong, since your legs are so long,
> To request you won't stay in Dumblane?'[15]

Lear's sense of his own eccentricity and isolation is quite apparent in these limericks. And while "they" often behave with unashamed rudeness, sounding (and looking, in the drawings) like a group of children teasing the new boy at school, "they" can clothe their rudeness in all the social amenities. What could be more cruelly polite than "their" request to the Old Person of Bow:

> There was an old person of Bow,
> Whom nobody happened to know;
> So they gave him some soap, and said coldly, 'We hope
> You will go back directly to Bow!'[16]

Here the social satire overshadows the nonsense element; if a person is not "known," society suspects even his personal cleanliness. People in the real world may not go so far as to offer him soap, but they might very well be tempted.

The individual, however, does not always take this abuse without striking back:

> There was an Old Man with a poker,
> Who painted his face with red oker
> When they said, 'You're a Guy!' he made no reply,
> But knocked them all down with his poker.[17]

He can often deliver a snappy comeback to silence their disapproval:

> There was an old person of Blythe,
> Who cut up his meat with a scythe;

When they said, 'Well! I never!'—he cried, 'Scythes for ever!'
That lively old person of Blythe.[18]

There was an old man in a garden,
Who always begged every-one's pardon;
When they asked him, 'What for?'—He replied 'You're a bore!
And I trust you'll go out of my garden.'[19]

When all else fails, he may simply leave, not in defeat, but in
triumph:

There was an Old Person of Basing,
Whose presence of mind was amazing;
He purchased a steed, which he rode at full speed,
And escaped from the people of Basing.[20]

Of course, one cannot know if the individual will find contentment in the place to which he escapes. Like Lear himself,
many of the limerick protagonists are compulsive wanderers. They
may be "of" a certain locality, but we meet them far from home.
("They" ask the Old Person to return *to* Bow.) Some run about
aimlessly, like the Old Man of Corfu:

There was an Old Man of Corfu,
Who never knew what he should do;
So he rushed up and down, till the sun made him brown,
That bewildered Old Man of Corfu.[21]

Many others have enough courage to cast aside conformity and
leave their homes for a time, but their resolve weakens, and they
decide to return:

There was an Old Person of Anerley,
Whose conduct was strange and unmannerly;
He rushed down the Strand, with a Pig in each hand,
But returned in the evening to Anerley.[22]

This character seems just to have lost his nerve, but others retreat
because of actual setbacks:

> There was an old person of Dundalk,
> Who tried to teach fishes to walk;
> When they tumbled down dead, he grew weary, and said,
> 'I had better go back to Dundalk!'[23]

The understatement of the final line is exquisite; we sympathize with the poor man despite the idiocy of his plan.

Nevertheless, the individual is not always the injured innocent, even if it takes very little to arouse the animosity of "them," and even if the universe can be cruel. Although Lear often felt himself to be the persecuted misfit, with those feelings resulting in outbursts of ill temper, he invariably came to apologize to his friends the next day, claiming himself entirely in the wrong. Sorting through his massive correspondence, Lear mused in a September 12, 1873, letter to Fortescue previously cited:

That either all my friends must be fools or mad; or, on the contrary, if they are not so, there must be more good qualities about this child than he ever gives or has given himself credit for possessing—else so vast and long continued a mass of kindness in all sorts of shapes could never have happened to him. Seriously it is one of the greatest puzzles to me, who am sure I am one of the most selfish and cantankerous brutes ever born, that heaps and heaps of letters—and these letters only the visible signs of endless acts of kindness, from such varieties of persons could have ever been written to me! Out of all I kept some specimens of each writer more or less interesting—four hundred and forty four individuals in all.

And just as he could see both sides of his relationships to these persons, who belonged to the influential classes of society that "they" are presumed to represent, so he could often empathize with "them" in their struggles to cope with his bizarre nonconformists.

While the punishment of the Old Man of Whitehaven seems needlessly harsh, several victims more or less invite their fates:

> There was an Old Person of Buda,
> Whose conduct grew ruder and ruder;

Till at last, with a hammer, they silenced his clamour,
By smashing that Person of Buda.[24]

Often "they" must endure the same kind of unprovoked rudeness
from the eccentric as he in other poems must endure from them,
a distinction being that "they" generally ask rude questions while
the individual generally gives rude answers. Perhaps the Young
Lady of Parma was justified in replying "Hum!" when "they said,
'Are you dumb?'"; but what justification had the Old Person of
Burton

Whose answers were rather uncertain;
When they said, 'How d'ye do?' he replied, 'Who are you?'
That distressing old person of Burton.[25]

Trying to communicate with many of the limerick protagonists
proves equally as uncertain and distressing:

There was an old person of Sestri,
Who sate himself down in the vestry,
When they said 'You are wrong!'—he merely said 'Bong!'
That repulsive old person of Sestri.[26]

No wonder "they" become frustrated and angry.

The last lines of the limericks do not always belong to the
eccentric. They often focus attention on the reaction of society,
explaining that the protagonist's behavior has "distressed" or
"vexed" or "perplexed" or "embarrassed" his neighbors. In some
cases the distress appears once more to indicate society's intolerance
of anything out of the ordinary:

There was an old man on the Border,
Who lived in the utmost disorder;
He danced with the cat, and made tea in his hat,
Which vexed all the folks on the Border.[27]

The Old Man's manner of living, one feels, should hardly concern,
let alone vex, his neighbors. And yet the choice of one man to live

in utmost disorder does in a symbolic way threaten the orderly well-being of all. In such verses as these, Lear invites us to see the guilt on both sides of the conflict.

While both sides thus share responsibility in creating the hostile climate between individual and society that many limericks portray, one should not overlook that smaller group of verses in which harmony rather than hostility characterizes the relations between the individual and "them." Sometimes the actions of the individual please "them," particularly if those actions involve dancing, playing an instrument, or giving some kind of artistic performance:

> There was an old person of Filey,
> Of whom his acquaintance spoke highly;
> He danced perfectly well, to the sound of a bell,
> And delighted the people of Filey.[28]

> There was a Young Lady of Tyre,
> Who swept the loud chords of a lyre;
> At the sound of each sweep, she enraptured the deep,
> And enchanted the city of Tyre.[29]

Or the individual may be in a position to offer help to his neighbors, like the Old Man of Dee-side, who offers "them" shelter under his "exceedingly wide" hat in case of a hail storm. More frequently, "they" find the individual in distress and come to his aid:

> There was an old person of Fife,
> Who was greatly disgusted with life;
> They sang him a ballad, And fed him on salad,
> Which cured that old person of Fife.[30]

Or "they" may try to warn him of some disaster "they" see as imminent:

> There was an Old Man at a casement,
> Who held up his hands in amazement;

When they said, 'Sir! you'll fall!' he replied, 'Not at all!'
That incipient Old Man at a casement.[31]

In some respects such warnings only confirm the conventionality
of society's point of view; "they" might indeed fall in such a
situation, but that doesn't mean the eccentric will necessarily do so.

And yet Lear's individuals do live recklessly, and if from one
perspective they appear as heroic rebel-martyrs against conformity,
from another they seem merely irrational, breaking the rules of
civilized society for no purpose whatsoever. The only safe general-
ization about the individual vis-á-vis "them" is that whether the
two coexist or quarrel, they differ qualitatively, remaining distinctly
separated types. This distinction results from a fundamental variance
in their respective approaches to life.

Lear perceives his characters as living in an environment of
occasional miracles and rather more frequent catastrophes. Prag-
matism, conformity, lack of imaginative daring—the attributes
"they" possess—provide a slim defense against the disasters, but a
creature who possesses only these qualities necessarily forfeits a
chance at the miracles. Lear's Old and Young Men, Persons, and
Ladies forsake the safety of the mean, ranging from utter despair
to wild delight (and in and out of the sympathies of their creator),
but do every now and then obtain something that "they" can never
have, what Thomas Byrom dubs "the sense of wonder": "We are
aroused from our customary indifference, and our curiosity is excited
to the point where we too stand on tiptoe . . . and look over the
lip of the intelligible world into the wonderful night beyond."[32]

The encounters with "them" may be the most characteristic
feature of Lear's limericks, but the protagonists participate in a
number of other kinds of relationships as well. Some have hus-
bands, wives, children, nieces, and cousins. As in life, children
in the limericks sometimes make their parents happy

There was an Old Man of Marseilles,
Whose daughters did nothing to please her;

> They caught several Fish, which they put in a dish,
> And sent to their Pa' at Marseilles.[33]

and at other times do not

> There was an old person of Pisa,
> Whose daughters did nothing to please her;
> She dressed them in gray, and banged them all day,
> Round the walls of the city of Pisa.[34]

No doubt as a reflection of Lear's own crowded and financially unstable early home life, many of the parents have extremely large families whom they must worry about feeding. The Old Man of Apulia feeds twenty sons on nothing but buns; the Old Person of Sparta feeds twenty-five sons and one daughter on snails (and then weighs his offspring in scales). But while these fathers have the situation well in hand, the fate of the Old Man of the East illustrates the other side of the case:

> There was an Old Man of the East,
> Who gave all his children a feast;
> But they all eat so much, and their conduct was such,
> That it killed that Old Man of the East.[35]

Without economy and discipline, the responsibilities of providing for a family can be fatal.

It is interesting to note that all these families picture only one parent. Nor do any of the married couples described in the limericks have children. No nuclear families of husband, wife, and children appear, perhaps because the brevity of the verse form could not accommodate them all. (Such families do appear in the longer poems.) Nevertheless, the limericks paint a picture of conjugal togetherness and parenthood as two separate activities, possibly revealing a subconscious dissociation of the two in the poet's mind. Furthermore, the marriages Lear describes are on the whole not happy. The wife of the Old Man of Peru bakes her spouse in a

stew, "by mistake," we are told, although the woman's expression
leaves some doubt as to the accidental nature of the proceedings.

Limerick: "Old Man of Peru"

The Old Man on some rocks imprisons his wife in a box. The
honeymooning couple of Hyde are menaced on the beach by a giant
crab. In the verse about the Old Person of Tartary, the wife appears
totally devoted to her husband:

> There was an Old Person of Tartary,
> Who divided his jugular artery;
> But he screeched to his wife, and she said, 'Oh, my life!
> Your death will be felt by all Tartary!'[36]

Yet if the marriage had been entirely blissful, would the husband
have "divided his jugular artery?" Lear was a man who spent his
entire adult life thinking he ought to marry, yet forever coming
up with excuses not to marry; the marriages in the limericks
reflect his ambivalent feelings about the state of matrimony.

Perhaps because of these doubts about family life, Lear has his limerick protagonists frequently form family groups, not with other human beings, but with animals. Lear had achieved his first successes as an artist with drawings of birds and animals, and particularly in the case of individuals who take up with avian friend, he delights in making the person resemble the animals with whom he associates:

Limerick: "Old Person of Crowle"

There was an old person of Crowle,
  Who lived in the nest of an owl;
  When they screamed in the nest, he screamed out with the rest,
That depressing old person of Crowle.[37]

In other poems, the Old Person of Hove studies tranquilly with the wrens and the rooks, the Old Person of Nice takes afternoon walks accompanied by a flock of geese, and the Old Man of Whitehaven dances his quadrille with a raven. In one limerick the relationship of the Old Man to a flock of birds visually parallels the fathers of Apulia and Sparta feeding their lined up offspring:

> There was an old man of Dumbree,
> Who taught little owls to drink tea;
> For he said, 'To eat mice, is not proper or nice,'
> That amiable man of Dumbree.[38]

Although the bond between birds and men is probably the strongest of any delineated in the limericks, Lear would not be Lear if he did not also portray some difficulties that might arise between them. Birds need nests, and they often tend to roost on long noses and in overgrown beards: . . . . . .

> There was an Old Man with a beard,
> Who said, 'It is just as I feared!—
> Two Owls and a Hen, four Larks and a Wren,
> Have all built their nests in my beard!'[39]

Or they may nip such noses and pluck out the hairs in such beards (and scalps) to line nests established elsewhere:

> There was an old man in a tree,
> Whose whiskers were lovely to see;
> But the birds of the air, pluck'd them perfectly bare,
> To make themselves nests in that tree.[40]

But the birds have a virtue, which they share with other animals and insects, that compensates for such moments of inconvenience. All have the capacity to serve as means of locomotion for the ever-roaming individuals:

> There was an old man whose despair
> Induced him to purchase a hare:
> Whereon one fine day, he rode wholly away,
> Which partly assuaged his despair.[41]

The impropriety and dangers of riding such beasts alarms "them," who frequently warn the individual of the likely consequences:

> There was an old man of Boulak,
> Who sate on a Crocodile's back;
> But they said, 'Tow'rds the night, he may probably bite,
> Which might vex you, old man of Boulak!'[42]

Typically, though, the only instance in which riding an animal actually proves hazardous occurs when the protagonist mounts a conventional beast of burden against which no one feels it necessary to warn him:

> There was an Old Man of Madras,
> Who rode on a cream-coloured ass;
> But the length of its ears, so promoted his fears,
> That it killed that Old Man of Madras.[43]

In all, animals appear in over one-fifth of the limericks, serving a variety of functions, some helpful, some antagonistic to the individual.[44] Insects tend to sting or perch vampirically on the neck. Dogs, which Lear feared in real life, are generally large and threatening. Cows charge at passers-by. Assorted beasts display a propensity to eat the protagonist's clothes. And men can also act antagonistically toward animals. The fish that frequently appear are often served up for supper. Despite the many happy relationships between men and animals, Lear does not idealize nature any more than he unequivocally condemns society or the family. But the behavior of animals, like that of men, is in the end unpredictable, and exceptions to all the above patterns can easily be discovered. Nor, as the drawings particularly emphasize, can we even be certain of the qualitative distinction between man and animal. In nonsense contradictions constantly threaten to merge, just as the Old Person of Crowle begins suspiciously to metamorphose into an actual owl.

Types of Eccentricity

Ultimately, however, the limerick protagonists become worthy of notice because of their inherent singularity, of which their

unusual interactions with "them," relatives, and the animal kingdom are merely expressions. So, many of the limericks are devoted
solely to commenting on those eccentric aspects of appearance or
behavior that make the individual remarkable. Some have not
chosen their eccentricity but have had it thrust upon them by
providence; they bear physical deformities. Paramount among these
abnormalities is the long and misshapen nose:

> There was a Young Lady whose nose,
> Was so long that it reached to her toes;
> So she hired an Old Lady, whose conduct was steady,
> To carry that wonderful nose.[45]

> There was an old man of West Dumpet,
> Who possessed a large nose like a trumpet;
> When he blew it aloud, it astonished the crowd,
> And was heard through the whole of West Dumpet.[46]

Lear was obsessed with the size of his own large nose, and the
repeated occurrence of obviously phallic noses throughout his work,
coupled with his sexually frustrated life, has kept Freudian critics
interested in his poetry. His characters also have overlong legs,
heads that are too small, eyes that are too big, and hair that grows
in strange configurations. While trying to compensate for these
deformities, they often make themselves even more ridiculous:

> There was an old person of Dutton,
> Whose head was so small as a button:
> So to make it look big, he purchased a wig,
> And rapidly rushed about Dutton.[47]

Of course, the abnormalities can sometimes prove useful, as in the
case of the Old Man of Coblenz whose immensely long legs take
him from Turkey to France "with one prance."
    George Orwell writes that the limerick protagonists all exude
"amiable lunacy," and Byrom talks about the Old Man and the
Young Lady as if all their incarnations were really the same

character. But Lear especially enjoys in creating these characters, I believe, the uniqueness of each. Nor does he regard them all as harmless and sympathetic cranks, as most critics have. Many are self-centered in either self-destructive or antisocial ways. Some display a passivity that almost amounts to catatonia:

> There was an Old Man of Moldavia,
> Who had the most curious behaviour;
> For while he was able, he slept on a table.
> That funny Old Man of Moldavia.[48]

> There was an old man of Hong Kong,
> Who never did anything wrong;
> He lay on his back, with his head in a sack,
> That innocuous old man of Hong Kong.[49]

In the latter verse Lear slyly implies that the only way to be sure of doing nothing "wrong" is to do nothing at all.

One discovers other characters sitting in solitude, trying to assuage some despair whose cause is never revealed; and occasionally, as in the case of the Old Man of Cape Horn, the misery proves unbearable:

> There was an Old Man of Cape Horn,
> Who wished he had never been born;
> So he sat on a chair, till he died of despair,
> That dolorous Man of Cape Horn.[50]

Such verses may reflect Lear's feelings in his own frequent spells of depression which he dubbed "the Morbids."

On the other hand, some of the individuals derive a reclusive pleasure from their isolation, appearing to have chosen to exclude themselves from ordinary social intercourse:

> There was an old person of Woking,
> Whose mind was perverse and provoking;
> He sate on a rail, with his head in a pail,
> That illusive old person of Woking.[51]

There was an old person of Bromley,
Whose ways were not cheerful or comely;
He sate in the dust, eating spiders and crust,
That unpleasing old person of Bromley.[52]

If the adjectives are to be believed, Lear heartily disapproves of those who voluntarily seek out loneliness. Yet even individuals who are perverse and provoking appear commendable next to those explosive personalities who express themselves in uncontrolled rage:

There was an old person of Newry,
Whose manners were tinctured with fury;
He tore all the rugs, and broke all the jugs
Within twenty miles' distance of Newry.[53]

The illustrations add to the frightening aspects of these persons by stressing their twisted mouths, dark brows, and hair standing on end.

Still, Lear does not deny some posititve features to his solitaires. Some happily exercise particular talents, winning favorable adjectives and pictorial representations from their author like the "eclectic" and vigorous Old Man of Port Grigor, who stands on his head, or the "amiable" and smiling Old Man of the Isles, who plays the fiddle. They may simply enjoy a contemplative life like the "scroobious and wily" Old Person of Philoe, who climbs a palm in calm weather to observe his native city, or the mysterious Young Person sitting in an unknown ditch to compose her "small treatise on history." Indeed, a sense of mystery surrounds many limerick protagonists. They know something that "they" (and we) never can; they may even have their own nonsense language to stress the incommunicable nature of that knowledge. The Old Man of Spithead announces from his window, "Fil-jomble, fil-jumble, Fil-rumble-come-tumble!" and the "laconic" Old Person of Wick restricts his vocabulary to "Tick-a-Tick, Tick-a-Tick;/Chickabee, Chickabaw."

In keeping with the two-sidedness of the limericks, however, inscrutable or mystic expressions of eccentricity are balanced by those involving the most fundamental human concerns, clothing and food. As children still do, the children for whom Lear composed his nonsenses doubtless spent a good portion of their time thinking about what they would wear and what they would eat if not under the control of parents and nurses who actually determined what they would dress in and what would be set on the table before them. Lear's protagonists fulfill childish fantasies of being able to don improper attire and eat exotic foods or strange combinations of food. In the matter of clothing, Lear is particularly fond of outlandish hats and wigs:

> There was a young person in red,
> Who carefully covered her head,
> With a bonnet of leather, and three lines of feather,
> Besides some long ribands of red.[54]

Such oversized head covering can come in handy during a sudden storm, as the Old Man of Dee-side demonstrates to his neighbors in a verse previously cited. Despite the shelter they receive in this instance, "they," representing conformist propriety in this as in all areas of life, disapprove of such vagaries in dress. Many of "their" customary rude remarks focus on the individual's lack of taste in his personal attire:

> There was an old person of Brill,
> Who purchased a shirt with a frill;
> But they said, 'Don't you wish, you may'nt look like a fish,
> You obsequious old person of Brill?'[55]

But Lear himself occasionally objects to extremes in dress (and in the drawing the Old Person of Brill *does* look like a fish); for donning a spickle-speckled sack, the Young Person of Crete earns the ominous label "ombliferous."

Just as the limerick protagonists wear what they like, despite society's disapproval, so they eat what they like. Over forty limericks deal with eating and drinking habits, with the illustrations often displaying the edibles in neatly labelled containers. From his Knowsley days onward, Lear most often met his young friends at mealtimes and composed limericks at the table or deposited non-senses on their plates to be discovered before the serving of the first course. So food naturally figures prominently in these verses.

But food in the limericks also has a symbolic function. The relationship between a person and food often serves to define his character. One learns that a person has a certain diet and nothing more, as if that information were sufficient to explain him:

> There was an Old Man of Vienna,
> Who lived upon Tincture of Senna;
> When that did not agree, he took Camomile Tea,
> That nasty Old Man of Vienna.[56]

In other instances the type of food is not as important as its manner of consumption. Gluttony brings nothing but trouble.[57] At the very least the overeater will grow fatter, like the "globular Person of Hurst." (This contented overeater is balanced by the "cautious old person of Dean," who dines on one pea and one bean because "More than that, would make me too fat.") More often the glutton becomes a disgusting monster, with the drawings showing him literally pushing food down his throat without stopping to chew, or even swallow. One of the more dependable cause and effect relationships in the unpredictable world of the limericks is that gluttony will generate its own punishment. The Old Person "whose habits/Induced him to feed upon rabbits" turns "perfectly green" after devouring eighteen of the animals in succession. He then has the good sense to "relinquish those habits." Others who do not learn the error of their ways pay dearly—by choking to death. This fate befalls the Old Man of the South with his "immoderate mouth" when he tries to swallow a full platter of fish, including the dish, all in one gulp; it also strikes the Young Person of Kew, "Whose virtues and vices were few," when she bolts down some hot paste "with blameable haste" and the Old Man of Calcutta:

Limerick: "Old Man of Calcutta"

Who perpetually ate bread and butter;
Till a great bit of muffin, on which he was stuffing,
Choked that horrid Old man of Calcutta.[58]

Gluttons seem to represent total self-absorption of a particularly odious kind to Lear. Of all the deaths that occur in the limericks, the poet relishes only these.

Lear does not, however, object to the pleasures derived from moderate dining. Individuals in despair often recover their composure if provided with a good meal:

> There was an old person of Pett,
> Who was partly consumed by regret;
> He sate in a cart, and ate cold apple tart,
> Which relieved that old person of Pett.[59]

In addition, willingness to feed others symbolizes love and caring in Lear's world. As noted above, descriptions of family relationships frequently portray the head of the household nourishing his offspring or animal companions. When "they" come to the aid of an individual in distress, "they" often succor him with gifts of food:

> There was an Old Person of Rheims,
> Who was troubled with horrible dreams;
> So, to keep him awake, they fed him with cake.
> Which amused that Old Person of Rheims.[60]

These symbolic patterns regarding food represent the most prominent feature of the limericks to carry over into Lear's longer poems and prose nonsense.

Another subject that carries over from the limericks to the other nonsense is the characters' fondness for music and dance, which they display in nineteen limericks.[61] Moreover, as John Lehmann notes: "In Lear's nonsense drawings again and again the chief characters point their toes as in ballet. There is a sense of dance everywhere in these drawings, as there is so often in the verses themselves."[62] Such poses well befit the freedom from conventional behavior that the limerick protagonists partake in. However, in many cases singing and dancing do not estrange the individual from the community as his other departures from convention often do. They rather serve to help him join it. As we have seen, the Young Lady of Tyre enchants all the people of her city with the sweep of her lyre, and the people of Filey applaud their fellow citizen for dancing to the sound of a bell. The protagonists also frequently cement their bonds with animals by singing to them or dancing with them. Many of Lear's greatest social successes occurred when he sat down at the piano at gatherings and sang his poems and those of others to the accompaniment of musical settings he had composed himself. This social utility of musical performance transfers into the world of the limericks.

Indeed, the gift of song functions similarly to the gift of food as an expression of affectionate caring, and the two sometimes appear in the same verses:

> There was an old person of Bray,
> Who sang through the whole of the day
> To his ducks and his pigs, whom he fed upon figs,
> That valuable person of Bray.[63]

In the verse about the Old Person of Fife quoted above we even see "them" making this gift as they "sang him a ballad and fed him on salad"—a rare and treasured moment of communion in the erratic relationship between the individual and society.

Not all the limericks deal with the individual and society, but all of them do contain a single individual whom the limerick attempts to define according to one set of terms or another: what does he look like? how does he behave? what does he say? how does he treat others? how do they treat him? what does he wear or eat? The limericks do not deal with abstract principles, general situations, or random observations. They all begin "there was an Old Person [Man, Lady]. . . ." They are all about *people,* considered one by one. To Lear, always conscious of being alone in the crowd, the odd man out, nothing else really mattered. Depending upon his mood, these distinctive individuals could appear as funny or sad, worthy of scorn or compassion, just as could those whose paths they crossed.

The Limericks as Nonsense

To return to the initial question, what then precisely is the nonsense element in the limericks? It takes two forms, that found in each verse considered separately, and in the limericks treated as a whole. Both forms involve at their base the Learian paradox, two contradictory ideas existing at the same time. The tensions, the double-sidedness, that these paradoxes generate differentiate the limericks from simple fantasy or comic incongruity—although these elements are present as well—and make the poems true nonsense. In the individual limericks I have noted the tension between the rigid verse form and the unconventionality of the content as well as between the final, judgmental adjective and the protagonist's described behavior. Byrom devotes several pages of his study to the many disparities between the message of the words and the message of the drawings. And within the lines themselves a general disjunction between cause and effect, event and reaction occurs, a prime characteristic of nonsense, whose first freedom is the freedom from logical causation.

When the Young Lady of Norway is squashed flat in a doorway, she merely exclaims "What of that?" The Old Man of the Nile "sharpened his nails with a file;/Till he cut off his thumbs, and said calmly, 'This comes—/Of sharpening one's nails with a file.'"[64] Several deaths are reported in a similarly detached tone:

> There was an Old Person of Ems,
> Who casually fell in the Thames;
> And when he was found, they said he was drowned,
> That unlucky Old Person of Ems.[65]

Here Lear plays on the literal derivation of *casually,* i.e. by accident, as well as the more figurative suggestion of the Old Person falling in without fuss or premeditation, rather like the Old Person of Cromer, who, growing stiff after reading Homer while standing on one leg, jumps over a cliff and is "concluded." One notes also that *"They said* he was drowned," as if the death might have been reversible without societal confirmation. "Their" word, not the water, kills. And while death and mutilation are thus received calmly, both "they" and the individual can be provoked into rage by the most inconsequential things.

Lack of cause and effect also appears when one considers the limericks as a body. The verses demonstrate that the desires of the individual and the needs of society and nature may either clash in irrational conflict or come into unexpected harmony. The terrifying thing is that you can never know which. Will your neighbors be vexed at you for dancing with the cat or applaud you for dancing to a bell? Will they smash you for playing a gong or grow enchanted by the sweep of your lyre? Herman Liebert notes that the limerick about the insomniac Old Man of the West, whom "they" set to spin on his nose and his chin, in manuscript concluded: "Which demolished that man of the West"; however, in the published version the final line read: "Which cured that Old Man of the West."[66] Fate is just that arbitrary in Lear, and the line between joy and disaster just that thin.

Lear accentuates the uncertainty of his world by teasing his readers with certainty. Predictable patterns do run through the limericks, e.g. "they" will react hostilely to eccentricity, gluttons will be punished, but just as one becomes confident in making such associations, the poet throws in an exception to upset them. Such final unpredictability is at base very frightening. In the limericks Lear underplays the terror of the situation through restraint of emotion in his presentation. He also divides his non-sense world into so many small pieces, with each verse containing a discrete, isolated permutation of the complex reality. Reading the limericks two or three at a time, as Lear's child friends did, causes only the comic side of the breakdown in causation to come through. When Lear moved on to less controlled poetic forms, however, the more melancholy aspects of the nonsense world became increasingly apparent, as the following chapter will demonstrate.

Chapter Three

The Longer Poems

General Characteristics

If, as the writer for the *Spectator* who reviewed Lear's nonsense books asserted, nonsense requires "a power of joyous rebellion against sense—of vital rebound from it,"[1] then the Lear of the longer poems was writing inferior nonsense, for his vital powers of joy and rebellion were certainly diminishing. And if, as Elizabeth Sewell believes, nonsense is a game that the forces of order in the mind play with the forces of disorder so that they may hold disorder in abeyance, then Lear was losing the emotional detachment necessary for playing the game.[2] Although it is going too far to say that Lear's longer poems do not qualify as nonsense, they do represent nonsense of a different kind. While many limerick protagonists choose to act eccentrically or to take on appearances that deviate from the expectations of society, a majority of the characters in the nonsense songs would love to fit into the crowd, only to have fate prevent them from doing so. Like Arnold's speaker in "Dover Beach," they stand on the shore and hear "the eternal note of sadness" coming in. Limericks that deal with catastrophes generally end as soon as the boom falls; the songs often begin with the catastrophe and explore the protagonist's attempts to adapt to reduced circumstances.

The "plots" of the nonsense songs do not vary as widely as do those of the limericks. Two themes, wandering and loss, predominate. Autobiographical parallels are clear. Lear had begun the limericks, and set their pattern, while still working at Knowsley, with many possibilities before him; the longer nonsense springs from the middle of his *Wanderjahre*, when the paradoxical contours of his trap had become all too familiar. But although the general mood of the longer poems is far more melancholy than that of the limericks, Lear still examines his themes from all possible angles. Poems about journeys describe either characters who escape an unsatisfactory status quo to seek freedom, adventure, and/or love or those whom the travelers have left behind. The poems scrutinize both those who leave and those who are left because Lear could alternately identify with each of these positions. He had escaped the confining atmosphere of England only to find himself deserted by the Lushingtons, Fortescues, and Congreves who could return home while he had to remain an exile. The losses that the poems portray may be either explicit loss of love and companionship or metaphorical deprivations of physical abilities, clothing, food, or mobility that express the poet's sense of his own imperfection and incompleteness.

In the longer poems the geography and the inhabitants of the nonsense world also differ somewhat from those in the limericks. While the limericks often verge on fantasy, Lear never wholeheartedly commits himself to it. All the places mentioned can be found on a map, the protagonists are all human beings (if outlandish ones), and animals do not talk. These conditions change in the nonsense songs. Some take place in the known world, but many of the travelers eventually arrive at the Great Gromboolian Plain or the Hills of the Chankly Bore, lands of Lear's invention. These lands do not belong to a separate fantasy universe, unrelated to our world, since, for example, the pelicans' daughter in "The Pelican Chorus" can fly there from a point of departure on the Nile. However, they represent a country—one might call it "nonsense land"—that Lear never discovered for all his journeying, an uncharted realm where contentment impossible in one's familiar surroundings may sometimes, although not always, be found. Its features recur from poem to poem, for the nonsense songs together constitute a related body of myth-making. Each separate verse explores a facet of nonsense land, and characters

who have a central role in one poem occasionally play a subsid-
iary role in another.

In keeping with the more fantastic setting, the characters rarely
qualify as humans, in even the dubious sense of humanness represented by the limerick protagonists. These poems feature either
anthropomorphized animals, personified inanimate objects, or
"humanoid" members of nonsense species such as the Dong,
Jumblies, Yonghy-Bonghy-Bó, Pobble, and Quangle Wangle. The
Discobboloses seem human enough, despite their name, until
Lear mentions in the sequel to their poem that Mrs. Discobbolos
is "octopod." Of all the longer poems humans appear only in
two minor verses, "The New Vestments" and "The Two Old
Bachelors," in the person of the Bó's beloved Lady Jingly Jones,
and as Lear himself in the autobiographical poems "How Pleasant to Know Mr. Lear" and "Incidents in the Life of My Uncle
Arly." All in all, the longer poems have far closer links to the
traditional nursery rhyme and fairy tale than do the limericks,
which create a specific atmosphere of nonsense for which previous analogs do not exist.

These changes that occur as one moves from limericks to nonsense songs possibly compensate for the loss of emotional distance
in the latter. The limericks reflect the paradoxes of Lear's life just
as strongly as do the other poems, but the presentation is abstract
and symbolic, and the disengagement of the poetic voice keeps
troublesome feelings under control. In the songs, however, the
parallels to Lear's actual experience cause him to separate himself
from his characters by dehumanizing them and setting them in
an imaginary landscape. The two groups of poems complement
one another and once more reflect the duality of Lear's art. They
stand in relation to one another as do the nonsense drawings to
the landscapes—the same world portrayed from two different perspectives. It is quite fitting, therefore, that the volumes that
contain Lear's limericks do not include any nonsense songs, and
the volumes that contain the longer poems, *Nonsense Songs*
(1871) and *Laughable Lyrics* (1877), contain no limericks.[3]

Nonsense Songs

Changes also occur between these two volumes of longer verse, for in *Nonsense Songs* the geography of nonsense land is sketchy, glimpsed from afar, and although the poems contain talking animals and animate household objects, only one, "The Jumblies," portrays any imaginary creatures. The loners who dominate the limericks and recur in some of the *Laughable Lyrics* do not appear here; except for the deserted "me" in "Calico Pie," all the poems feature pairs or groups of creatures setting out on journeys together. These verses explore Lear's need to travel, rather than emphasize the loneliness he often felt while traveling. In fact, as a group these first nonsense songs share a greater consistency of theme than any other related group of Learian verses. Each one concerns protagonists who become dissatisfied with life at home and set off for new surroundings. Then Lear, in his typical multiplicitous manner, examines in turn all the variables such a basic situation might entail.

The three most closely connected poems, "The Owl and the Pussy-cat," "The Duck and the Kangaroo," and "The Daddy Long-Legs and the Fly," had previously appeared together in the American journal *Young Folks* in 1870. Each describes two disparate creatures coming together as travel companions and details their journeys. The motivations for the travel differ in each case, however. The owl and the pussy-cat go on a courtship voyage; they change rapidly from companions to lovers to husband and wife. The kangaroo seems a wonderer by profession, and the duck joins him out of boredom with its home pond. The daddy long-legs and the fly have become misfits in formerly comfortable surroundings and flee to nonsense land as companions in misfortune, creating a new life in reduced circumstances. So in the three poems the mood at journey's end changes from festive happiness to less ecstatic contentment to resigned sadness.

"The Owl and the Pussy-cat," probably Lear's best known poem, is also one of his happiest.[4] Along with "The Jumblies" it illustrates those occasional miracles that every now and then replace the disasters that the arbitrary and paradoxical fortune of Lear's universe usually brings on. The title pair, to be sure, do not hurl themselves recklessly at fate as do some of the limerick characters. They prudently set out well-provisioned and financed: "They took some honey, and plenty of money,/Wrapped up in a five-pound note."[5] They also pay attention to social proprieties. Pussy exclaims: "O let us be married! too long we have tarried," but because a proper wedding requires a ring, they tarry another year and a day in search of one. The "too long we have tarried" is itself ambiguous. Does Pussy mean that two lovers should not sail for very long together in a "beautiful pea-green boat" without benefit of clergy? Or does "married" mean "consummated," synonymous in a respectable Victorian vocabulary? Have they restrained their passion for too long? The time spent searching for the ring implies commitment to social duty on the one hand and further damage to reputation and further frustration of passion on the other—Lear's typical paradoxical trap.

However, the difficulties disappear when the lovers finally leave our world and arrive at "the land where the Bong-tree grows." A pig with the desired ring in his nose miraculously appears, willing to sell it for only one shilling of the substantial sum wrapped up in the five-pound note. And a "Turkey who lives on the hill" is immediately at hand to perform the marriage ceremony. Since the sharing of food always cements loving relationships in Lear, the poet details the contents of the wedding feast, "mince and slices of quince," eaten with a "runcible spoon," bearing one of Lear's favorite nonsense adjectives. Then comes the epiphany:

> And hand in hand, on the edge of the sand,
>   They danced by the light of the moon,
>   The moon,
>   The moon,
>   They danced by the light of the moon.

Here the positive values of song and dance transfer over from the limericks; such scenes will occur again and again in the longer poems.

The shore and moonlight also figure prominently and frequently in the settings of nonsense land, for both encompass the contradictions of that land. The shore mediates between settled ground and wandering sea; it is a place from which one embarks, upon which one starts a new life, and where one may be left behind by love. Moonlight combines brightness with darkness, may suggest magic or melancholy. In this poem, and many of the others, it is certainly magic, with the joy of owl and pussy-cat emphasized by the energetic finale of the refrain in which "moon," like the words that end each of the other stanzas, is repeated four times.

Trouble never enters the world of "The Owl and the Pussy-cat," but its absence may result because Lear looks only at the culminating miracle and not at the origins of the two creatures' love or the causes of their setting out on their voyage. "The Owl and the Pussy-cat went to sea/In a beautiful pea-green boat"; this is all we know. Could their love perhaps not flourish on land? Did some equivalent of "them" decide that owls and pussy-cats should not mate (as indeed they do not in nature)? Moreover some sexual confusion occurs in the poem, since Lear never denotes either owl or pussy-cat by a male or female pronoun,[6] although he describes the pig as definitely male, "with a ring at the end of *his* nose" (italics mine). Subconsciously, perhaps, Lear is leaving the lovers' respective sexes ambiguous, and making them of different species, in order to portray his conflicting desires for both the security of conventional marriage and, the deeper need, for love from his closest male friends.

In the limericks one never thinks to question the motivations of the protagonists; they all live quite beyond the pale of psychology. The longer poems, however, while portraying a nonsensical lack of logic in the causation of events, deal with character in a more realistic fashion. Because Lear in most of the other travel poems describes precisely what set the characters off on their journeys, the lack of such information in this poem creates at least a suspicion that if the information had not been suppressed, it might have compromised the joyous tone of "The Owl and the Pussy-cat."

Lear's second pair of travelers, the duck and the kangaroo, do not actually set off on their travels until four lines from the end of the poem. If Lear reveals very little about the reasons and preparations for the voyage of the owl and the pussy-cat, he devotes this verse to little else. The journey itself seems almost anticlimactic. "The Duck and the Kangaroo" primarily expresses the theme of symbiotic cooperation in adapting to circumstances that characterizes several of the longer poems, but that "The Owl and the Pussy-cat" touches on only briefly. The relationship of the two companions differs substantially from that of the owl and the pussy-cat, in that the respective attributes of duck and kangaroo complement a lack in the other, while the owl and the pussy-cat, equal partners in love, seek from outside help in meeting a shared need. The duck and the kangaroo need each other's aid in much the same way that both owl and pussy-cat need the aid of the pig and the turkey.

The duck is the thinker of the pair, the prime mover in their adventure, who gives direction to the aimless wanderings of the kangaroo. Although the poem is structured as a dialogue, with each stanza beginning either "Said the Duck" or "Said the Kangaroo," the duck originates and dominates the conversation. It—once again the sex of the characters is not specified—has an expansive imagination that has been frustrated because of its confinement to "this nasty pond" where "my life is a bore." The kangaroo, on the other hand, has the physical capability to "hop!/Over the fields and the water too,/As if you never would stop!"[7] So the duck asks for a ride, promising to "sit quite still, and say nothing but 'Quack,'/The whole of the long day through!"—although the aggressive, voluble confidence it displays throughout the poem casts doubt on how well it might keep such a promise. And directly following its promise of reticence, it proceeds to set the itinerary: "And we'd go to the Dee, and the Jelly Bo Lee,/ Over the land, and over the sea."

Although the kangaroo is a timid, old-maidish sort—another side of Lear, the hypochondriacal traveler—who stands to gain little from the partnership, it graciously tells the duck that its companionship "might bring me luck." However, the prospect of the duck's "unpleasantly wet and cold" feet on its back does not delight the kangaroo, and it fears that rheumatism may result from their touch. But the seemingly impulsive duck has in fact figured everything out carefully in advance:

> Said the Duck, 'As I sate on the rocks,
> I have thought over that completely,
> And I bought four pairs of worsted socks
> Which fit my web-feet neatly.
> And to keep out the cold I've bought a cloak,
> And every day a cigar I'll smoke,
> All to follow my own dear true
> Love of a Kangaroo!'

So they leave "all in the moonlight pale" for another Learian epiphany:

> So away they went with a hop and a bound,
> And they hopped the whole world three times round;
> And who so happy,—O who,
> As the Duck and the Kangaroo?. [*sic*]

It is rather a shock to hear the duck, who has approached their joint trip as a prudently conceived business proposition, suddenly declare his or her passion for "my own dear true love of a Kangaroo." Indeed, the sexual content in this poem differs far more from conventionalized courtship than does the romance of the owl and the pussy-cat, which is nonsensical only in the difference of their species and the uncertainty about their respective genders. "The Duck and the Kangaroo" shares these confusions, but it adds some more ambiguous Freudian undercurrents. The poem contains no masculine or feminine pronouns at all. Since the duck

makes all the plans and advances and wears a cloak and smokes
cigars, it would seem to be masculine. Yet Byrom asserts that
the duck is female and that "the joke is: how funny to have a
timid kangaroo and a bossy duck."[8] He provides no evidence
for making the assumption, but one imagines the illustrations may
have influenced him. With the duck straddling it, the kangaroo's
tail, formerly trailing limply on the ground, juts out straight and
erect; the visual phallic suggestions are quite strong. And the

"The Duck and the Kangaroo"

kangaroo's fears of the unpleasantly wet and cold feet of the duck
likewise suggest a sexual image, this time one of aversion in which
the kangaroo seems female rather than male. It feels safe to proceed only after the proper prophylactic precautions have been
taken. But whatever its indications of Lear's uneasiness about
physical sexual contact and his ambivalence about sexual identity,
"The Duck and the Kangaroo" does not concern itself primarily with romance. It deals with the need to escape dull routine
and the various compromises and adaptations that are the price of

freedom. Even more than the owl and the pussy-cat, the duck and the kangaroo depart from the impulsive model of the wilder limerick protagonists to become the prudent tourists abroad. They doubtless closely resemble Lear and Giorgio on a painting expedition.

The third verse of this group, "The Daddy Long-legs and the Fly," has nothing to do with the need for romance or adventure. Since love is not at issue here, Lear makes both characters decidedly male; he gives both the title "Mr." and uses "he" frequently to refer to both. The poem is the first of several describing the loss of joys once possessed, of happy days that are no more. The two companions, despite a long sea voyage "far, and far away . . . across the silent main" to the great Gromboolian plain, end as they began, playing battlecock and shuttledoor. No magic moonlight bathes the cold, dreary shore upon which they meet or the vast empty plain to which they flee.

Technically the verse advances beyond the simple rhyme schemes, thumping rhythms, and childish diction—the nursery-rhyme quality—of "The Owl and the Pussy-cat" and "The Duck and the Kangaroo." Here the stanza form is longer, the pace slower, and the rhyme scheme for each stanza a complex *a b c, b d e f e, g g, h h*. These changes combine to create a subdued and sadder mood. As the action comes back around to the initial situation, so the poetic structure is generally symmetrical. A first narrative stanza is followed by five dialogue stanzas that alternate between the two speakers, as in "The Duck and the Kangaroo." The sixth stanza varies from the pattern by beginning with four lines of narration and continuing with eight lines of dialogue spoken by the two insects in unison. A seventh narrative stanza, parallel to the first, concludes the poem.

Lear may have made that sixth stanza structurally distinct from the others because it contains the heart of his message, to which he wants to call attention:

> So Mr. Daddy Long-legs
> And Mr. Floppy Fly

> Sat down in silence by the sea,
>   And gazed upon the sky.
> They said, 'This is a dreadful thing!
> The world has all gone wrong,
> Since one has legs too short by half,
>   The other much too long!
> One never more can go to court,
> Because his legs have grown too short;
> The other cannot sing a song,
> Because his legs have grown too long!'[9]

Unlike the previous travelers, and those that succeed them in *Nonsense Songs*, the daddy long-legs and the fly have not become discontented with life at home and so sought greener pastures; life has, so to speak, become discontented with them and has arbitrarily altered them so that they no longer fit into a formerly comfortable existence—the world *has* all gone wrong. The poem portrays a situation in which nothing quite fits together. The two insects meet at an awkward time ("it was too soon to dine") of day, upon a summer's afternoon when, however, "the wind was rather cold." None of the many colors mentioned in the poem match. The daddy long-legs is dressed in brown and gray, the fly in blue and gold, the king and queen of the court in red and green. The sails of the companions' boat are pink and gray, not the "pea-green" of the sails in Lear's poems that tell of happier voyages. Even the mutual pastime they can still share and engage in, a game of badminton, has had its name scrambled from battledore and shuttlecock to "battlecock and shuttledoor." Most tragically, although the afflictions of each would work to the advantage of the other, they have no way to exchange them. They cannot form a symbiotic unit as can the duck and the kangaroo. So their resort to nonsense land "with one spongetaneous cry" in a providentially appearing boat is an act taken by exiles rather than seekers. The silent timelessness evoked in the closing lines suggests a limbolike, purgatorial existence:

> They sailed across the silent main,
>   And reached the great Gromboolian plain;

> And there they play for evermore
> At battlecock and shuttledoor.

In a poem whose prevailing mood is one of estrangement, the game itself is one that separates the players with a net.

The subdued tone of "The Daddy Long-legs and the Fly" prefigures the melancholy strains of the misnamed *Laughable Lyrics*[10] such as "The Dong with a Luminous Nose," "The Pobble Who Has No Toes," and "The Courtship of the Yonghy-Bonghy-Bò." And even the two preceding, happier voyage poems lack the exuberant, devil-take-the-hindmost nonconformity that often appears in the limericks. But Lear had not quite finished with the limerick spirit of nonsense, which returns in two of the *Nonsense Songs*, "The Jumblies," and "The Nutcrackers and the Sugar-Tongs."

"The Jumblies" could serve as a compendium of the many sides of the relationship between "them" and the limerick protagonists. The poem begins with a spirited disregard for conventional wisdom:

> They went to sea in a Sieve, they did,
>   In a Sieve they went to sea:
> In spite of all their friends could say,
> On a winter's morn, on a stormy day,
>   In a Sieve they went to sea!
> And when the Sieve turned round and round,
> And every one cried, 'You'll all be drowned!'
> They called aloud, 'Our Sieve ain't big,
> But we don't care a button! we don't care a fig!
>   In a Sieve we'll go to sea!'[11]

It is as if several Old Persons had banded together in a type of corporate eccentricity, impossible in the fragmented "real" world of the limericks, but achievable in the "far and few" lands where the Jumblies live and where even normal people have green heads and blue hands. The Jumblies' friends embody the concerns "they" frequently express for both Philistine propriety and the genuine dangers that the eccentric braves:

'O won't they be soon upset, you know!
For the sky is dark, and the voyage is long,
And happen what may, it's extremely wrong
In a Sieve to sail so fast!'

Erika Leimert remarks that the friends' warnings resemble those
given to most explorers and that the Jumblies themselves represent
"aller derer, die unbekümmert um das Urteil der anderen, sich
in das Unbekannte hinauswagen, unerschrocken das scheinbar
Unmögliche versuchen" (all those who, unconcerned with the
judgments of others, set forth into the unknown, unafraid to
attempt the seemingly impossible.)[12] Lear, however, realizes that
the friends have a good deal of sense on their side when they
forecast shipwreck for a leaky sieve. For the Jumbly vessel is not a
magic sieve that does not take in water. Lear pushes his paradox
to its limits when he reports "The water it soon came in, it
did,/The water it soon came in."

The Jumblies perceive the water as threatening only to make
their feet wet, not to sink them. So they wrap their feet in pinky
paper and climb into a crockery jar for the night. And in this poem
faith and ingenuity carry the day; their feet stay dry and the sieve
illogically stays afloat. The Jumblies successfully sail to the distant
Western Sea. Lear parallels their nonsense view of the adventure,
characterized by the elevation of individual instinct over all other
considerations, with the previously cited sense of the friends:

And each of them said, 'How wise we are!
Though the sky be dark, and the voyage be long,
Yet we never can think we were rash or wrong,
While round in our Sieve we spin!'

In "The Jumblies" all the potential catastrophes that inform the
Learian universe miraculously vanish, just as the voyagers' seemingly ineffective methods for dealing with the incoming water
prove to be just the thing. The singsong of the refrain has an
incantatory quality that keeps all harm away.

The Jumbly voyage is so magical that they reach their epiphany before reaching their destination. Moonlight and song accompany the very first night of their travels:

> They whistled and warbled a moony song
> To the echoing sound of a coppery gong,
>   In the shade of the mountains brown.
> 'O Timballo! How happy we are,
> When we live in a sieve and a crockery-jar,
> And all night long in the moonlight pale,
> We sail away with a pea-green sail,
>   In the shade of the mountains brown!'

The final element of Learian communion, food, appears when they land and purchase

> . . . an Owl, and a useful Cart,
> And a pound of Rice, and a Cranberry Tart,
>   And a hive of silvery Bees.
> And they bought a Pig, and some green Jack-daws,
> And a lovely Monkey with lollipop paws,
> And forty bottles of Ring-Bo-Ree,
>   And no end of Stilton Cheese.

The enumeration of incongruous items, a characteristic of nonsense,[13] suggests the limericks once more. One almost hears "There was an Old Man with a Cart, who purchased a Cranberry Tart" or "There was an Old Person of Dawes, who had a monkey with Lollipop paws."

Most of the travelers in the limericks, and in Lear's other poems, either leave home for good to find happiness (or at least lessening of pain) or return home defeated in some way. But the Jumblies, after twenty years or more, all come back in triumph, having grown tall and conquered "the Lakes, and the Torrible Zone,/And the hills of the Chankly Bore." Lear then incorporates into the conclusion of the poem another, and the rarest, facet of the limericks: the coming together of romantic nonconformists and careful society. For upon the Jumblies' return the friends display no bitter-

ness at seeing their gloomy prophecies refuted; rather they make
an offering of food. Instead of adhering rigidly to their prosaic
principles, they convert enthusiastically to the Jumbly philosophy:

> And they drank their health, and gave them a feast
> Of dumplings made of beautiful yeast;
> And every one said, 'If we only live,
> We too will go to sea in a Sieve,—
> To the hills of the Chankly Bore!'

Although the "if we only live" darkens the ending somewhat,
implying that the friends either retain some doubts about the safety
of the voyage or, more likely, have waited too long to trust in themselves and throw off conventional restraints, "The Jumblies"
nevertheless stands as one of Lear's most optimistic and joyous
works. Because, however, Lear could always see the dark side
of happiness (and conversely the lighter side of disaster) he does
not leave the euphoria of the poem uncontradicted. Therefore, in
Laughable Lyrics, as we shall see, he uses the Jumbly chorus and
the Jumbly voyage in "The Dong" to reveal that their triumphal
return does not represent an unalloyed happy ending for everyone.

"The Nutcrackers and the Sugar-Tongs" does not even attempt
to realize the communal joy of "The Jumblies," but it shares
with the former poem a reversion to the limerick conflict between
"them" and eccentrics who fly in the face of conventional behavior for their kind. The heroes here are inanimate table accessories, who, like the duck, detest a boring and circumscribed
existence:

> 'Must we drag on this stupid existence for ever,
> 'So idle and weary, so full of remorse,—
> 'While every one else takes his pleasure, and never
> 'Seems happy unless he is riding a horse?'[14]

Since their long legs, unlike those useless limbs of the daddy
long-legs and fly, are "so aptly constructed," they decide to join

"everyone else" for a ride. When the nutcracker, who has originated the plan, experiences a moment of doubt ('Shall we try? Shall we go? Do you think we are able?'), the tongs settles the matter with a decisive "Of course!" As in "The Jumblies," faith in one's ability to accomplish a goal generates the ability to accomplish it. In an instant the adventurers leave the house, enter the stable, mount up, and ride away. Of course, "they," the respectable kitchen accessories, voice their disapproval, in a passage that echoes the nursery rhyme "Hey Diddle Diddle":

> The whole of the household was filled with amazement,
> The Cups and the Saucers danced madly about,
> The Plates and the Dishes looked out of the casement,
> The Saltcellar stood on his head with a shout,
> The Spoons with a clatter looked out of the lattice,
> The Mustard-pot climbed up the Gooseberry Pies,
> The Soup-ladle peeped through a heap of Veal Patties,
> And squeaked with a ladle-like scream of surprise.

Despite their intention to join everyone else, mobility and freedom so exhilarate the nutcrackers and the tongs that they leave the mundane world behind by galloping away to—where else in Lear?—the "beautiful shore." They decide, "We will never go back any more." As their snapping and cracking fade away, the poet reports, "And they never came back."[15] The emphatic finality of the escape resembles that of the inhabitants of Basing and Rimini in the limericks:

> There was an Old Person of Basing,
> Whose presence of mind was amazing;
> He purchased a steed, which he rode at full speed,
> And escaped from the people of Basing.[16]

> There was an old person of Rimini,
> Who said, 'Gracious! Goodness! O Gimini!'
> When they said, 'Please be still!' she ran down a hill,
> And was never more heard of at Rimini.[17]

Such might have been Lear's mood as he left England on the first trip to Rome.

Lear does not wait for a later volume to explore an unhappier side of the situation portrayed in "The Nutcrackers and the Sugar-Tongs." In the poem that directly follows it in *Nonsense Songs*, "Calico Pie," the triumphant exclamation, "And they never came back," becomes a lament "They never came back to me." While all the preceding poems deal with a small group of adventurers who run away from the conventional crowd, this song, one of the few works Lear wrote in the first person, portrays a "me," an individual of unspecified age, sex, or species, whom the whole animal kingdom, and by implication, the whole world, has abandoned. Each of the four stanzas has precisely the same structure, beginning with "Calico" combined with a monosyllable, then describing in turn "little Birds," "little Fish," "little Mice," and "Grasshoppers," who engage in their normal forms of loco-motion, perform some other activity, and then never return to the speaker, e.g.:

> Calico Jam,
> The little Fish swam,
> Over the syllabub sea,
> He took off his hat,
> To the Sole and the Sprat,
> And the Willeby-wat,—
> But he never came back to me!
> He never came back!
> He never came back!
> He never came back to me![18]

The rhymes are lively, and the refrain with its fourfold repe-tition resembles that of "The Owl and the Pussy-cat," but the poem describes desertion and isolation rather than union. Although the other songs reflect Lear's restlessness with settled domesticity, "Calico Pie" delineates the wanderer's loneliness. Because he makes it a converse of his travel poems, one might conclude that Lear sees his loneliness resulting from his decision to wander.

The "me" may also represent those he had left behind in England, particularly his sister Ann, and he perhaps feels his loneliness is a punishment for running out on them. In any event, his sympathies were shifting, and in *Laughable Lyrics* his attention leaves the voyager to look at the individual who "starts in a paradise, isolated, only to end up in a paradise, doubly deserted."[19]

In the remaining three poems in *Nonsense Songs*, however, Lear takes a look at those who willingly live settled domestic lives and whose travels involve only afternoon excursions. "Mr. and Mrs. Spikky Sparrow" represents Lear's one attempt to portray a happy family in which mother, father, and children live together in an atmosphere of mutual concern and affection; the Sparrows inhabit a wish-fulfillment household Lear had never had and would never have. Touching in its naive assumptions about what constitutes domestic happiness, the poem nevertheless represents a failure of imagination on Lear's part because such a situation was totally outside his emotional experience. It is the only Lear poem that is cloying in the same way as much inferior Victorian children's literature, particularly the refrain with its "Twikky wikky wikky wee,/Wikky bikky twikky tee" and other "ikky" variations. The tetrameter couplets are technically uninspired.[20]

As her husband sits on a nearby branch, Mrs. Sparrow is "A-making of an insect pie" and singing to amuse "her little children five/In the nest and all alive"[21]—unlike the majority of the twenty-one little Lears. But Mrs. Sparrow is concerned about her husband's coughing and sneezing, brought on by his failure to wear a hat. Mr. Sparrow takes no umbrage at her wifely nagging; on the contrary, he thanks her effusively:

> Mr. Spikky said, 'How kind,
> 'Dear! you are, to speak your mind!
> 'All your life I wish you luck!
> 'You are! you are! a lovely duck!

And now that the subject has come up, the husband remarks that her health too has been suffering from lack of a bonnet.

Mrs. Sparrow's wording of her concern, however, indicates that the pair want to wear hats for reasons beyond the simple warding off of colds and neuralgia: "No one stays out all night long/Without a hat: I'm sure it's wrong!" "Wrong" here has the same double meaning, of both unhealthy and socially improper, something "no one" does, that it has when the friends of the Jumblies use it. Therefore, the two birds decide to dress in the height of fashion in order to "look and feel/Quite galloobious and genteel!" Lest they be too extravagant, though, they choose to buy second hand in "Moses' wholesale shop." They return to the excited compliments of their offspring:

> Their children cried, 'O Ma and Pa!
> 'How truly beautiful you are!'
> Said they, 'We trust that cold or pain
> 'We shall never feel again!
> 'While, perched on tree, or house, or steeple,
> 'We now shall look like other people.'

This rejoicing over conformity puts the Sparrows light years away from the Jumblies or the limerick eccentrics in their bizarre outfits. Lear never really approves of the values that "they" hold, and that the Sparrows wish to emulate, but he realizes that one can avoid much heartache—"cold or pain"—by going along with "other people." In "Mr. and Mrs. Spikky Sparrow," a poem oozing contentment, he for once gives "them" their due.

The poet casts a more cynical eye at cozy domesticity in the two verses that conclude *Nonsense Songs*, "The Broom, the Shovel, the Poker, and the Tongs" and "The Table and the Chair." These return to the world of household implements introduced in "The Nutcrackers and the Sugar-Tongs." The former begins as a courtship poem like "The Owl and the Pussy-cat." As two couples, Mr. Tongs and Mrs. Broom, Mr. Poker and Miss Shovel, take a coach ride in the park, all four sing a song, generally a sign of loving togetherness in Lear. And the Poker's serenade, which combines an offer of food with song, reinforces the impression of a love poem:

'O Shovely so lovely!' the Poker he sang,
  'You have perfectly conquered my heart!
'Ding-a-dong! Ding-a-dong! If you're pleased with my song,
  'I will feed you with cold apple tart!²²

But the third stanza, sung by the tongs, turns into a lament. Mrs. Broom "doesn't care about me a pin." He suspects that she objects to his thinness and long legs, characteristics unavoidable in a pair of tongs. While the sugar-tongs found its shape advantageous for making a mounted escape, the long legs of this pair of fireplace tongs are a liability, as were the elongated limbs of the daddy long-legs, and, his self-caricatures reveal, as Lear thought his own lanky legs to be. The tongs addresses his love bitterly:

'Ah! why don't you heed my complaint!
'Must you needs be so cruel, you beautiful Broom,
'Because you are covered with paint?
  'Ding-a-dong! Ding-a-dong!
  'You are certainly wrong!'

Here "wrong" carries none of the ambiguity of its use in "The Jumblies" and "Mr. and Mrs. Spikky Sparrow"; it is a heartfelt protestation against injustice.

The response of the two ladies ends any speculation about the song being a love poem:

Mrs. Broom and Miss Shovel together they sang,
  'What nonsense you're singing today!'
Said the Shovel, 'I'll certainly hit you a bang!'
Said the Broom, 'And I'll sweep you away!'

The broom and the shovel significantly repudiate nonsense itself. At this point the coachman, "perceiving their anger with pain," quickly drives them home. There, no doubt on the hearth where they perform their household duties, "they put on the kettle, and little by little,/They all became happy again." The poet then suddenly intrudes with "there's an end of my song," even though the previous songs in the poem had been specifically attributed to the characters. Perhaps he identifies himself with them at the end in order to make the reader accept the validity of the dubious reconciliation. Even if one does believe that the four become "happy" again, their happiness can surely comprise only an absence of overt strife, not the joy achieved by the owl and the pussy-cat or the Jumblies. The reversals of symbols of joy from the happier poems reveal that love may flourish in nonsense land but not on the homely hearth.

The first two stanzas of "The Table and the Chair" contain a statement made by the table to the chair and the chair's reply, a dialogue structure similar to that of "The Duck and the Kangaroo" and "The Daddy Long-legs and the Fly." Like the duck, the table finds life confining and proposes travel as a cure:

> 'You can hardly be aware,
> 'How I suffer from the heat,
> 'And from chilblains on my feet!
> 'If we took a little walk,
> 'We might have a little talk!
> 'Pray let us take the air!'[23]

And like the kangaroo the chair demurs; it moreover believes the plan impossible of execution:

> 'Now you *know* we are not able!
> 'How foolishly you talk,
> 'When you know we *cannot* walk!'

As in several of the preceding poems, however, faith in oneself can work miracles; the table persuades its companion that "it can do no harm to try." Although "slowly" and with a "cheerful bumpy sound," they succeed in walking around town, to the amazement of all.

Up to this point, "The Table and the Chair" closely resembles "The Nutcrackers and the Sugar-Tongs." But these adventurers do not, like the nutcrackers and tongs, disappear over the horizon, nor do they go around the world three times like the duck and kangaroo. As in "The Broom, the Shovel, the Poker, and the Tongs," Lear reverses a pattern established in oher poems, for the table and chair become hopelessly and helplessly lost. They finally must pay a duck, mouse, and beetle to guide them home. These creatures serve the same function as the coachman in the preceding poem and illustrate the characters' loss of control over their own destinies. Once safely home, the table and chair stage a Learian epiphany with food and dancing:

> 'What a lovely walk we've taken!
> Let us dine on Beans and Bacon!'
> So the Ducky, and the leetle
> Browny-Mousy and the Beetle
> Dined, and danced upon their heads
> Till they toddled to their beds.

None of Lear's other successful adventurers ever cuts his festivities short to "toddle" off to bed. The quality of the dash for freedom has diminished radically. As Byrom notes: "They are really strays and belong at home. When the animals rescue them, they congratulate each other like tourists who have been badly frightened but do not care to admit it to each other."[24] Their flying in the face of probability has far more mixed results than in the other nonsense songs and in the limericks. And in his later long poems Lear would abandon this reckless attitude or else show it having dreadful consequences.

Laughable Lyrics

The eccentric spirit of the limericks has its last gasp in a little-known poem, "The New Vestments." The protagonist is an "old man in the Kingdom of Tess/Who invented a purely original dress." With their designation of an old man from a specific locality who did something out of the ordinary, these first two lines strongly suggest the opening of a limerick. The "original dress," which combines dead mice, rabbit skins, and other skins of uncertain origin ("but it is not known whose") with garments composed of all manner of edible substances, resembles the outlandish costumes of many limerick protagonists. One thinks in particular of the old man of Blackheath:

> Whose head was adorned with a wreath,
> Of lobsters and spice, pickled onions and mice,
> That uncommon old man of Blackheath.[25]

But this poem, with five stanzas and forty-three lines of heroic couplets, provides far more space for detailed reflection on the phenomenon of bizarre dress than does the brief, prescribed limerick verse form. Although the fate of the new vestments parallels that of the spinach shawl worn by the young lady of Greenwich: "But a large spotty Calf, bit her shawl quite in half,/Which alarmed that young lady of Greenwich,"[26] the emotional effects of the incidents, and their magnitude, differ completely. The young lady merely suffers through an alarming experience, while the old man of Tess undergoes a harrowing, nightmare variation on "The Emperor's New Clothes":

> He had walked a short way, when he heard a great noise,
> Of all sorts of Beasticles, Birdlings, and Boys;—
> And from every long street and dark lane in the town
> Beasts, Birdles, and Boys in a tumult rushed down.
> Two Cows and a half ate his Cabbage-leaf Cloak;—
> Four Apes seized his Girdle, which vanished like smoke;—
> Three Kids ate up half of his Pancaky Coat,—
>
> .   .   .   .
>
> He tried to run back to his house, but in vain,
> For Scores of fat Pigs came again and again;—
> They rushed out of stables and hovels and doors,—
> They tore off his stockings, his shoes, and his drawers;—
> And now from the housetops with screechings descend,
> Striped, spotted, white, black, and gray Cats without end,
> They jumped on his shoulders and knocked off his hat,—
> When Crows, Ducks, and Hens made a mincemeat of that;—
>
> .   .   .   .

They swallowed the last of his Shirt with a squall,—
Whereon he ran home with no clothes on at all.[27]

It is easy to forget that the attackers are only eating up the food-constituted clothes; the episode suggests both rape and cannibalism. The old man seems about to be devoured himself by a horde of ravening predators, who suggest all those grotesque limerick gluttons. This time, however, the gluttons do not choke or become ill but completely rout the milder eccentric. Due to the overall absurdity of the situation, the piling up of details, and the impossible magnitude of the attack force, the poem generates considerable humor. (It closely resembles a Dr. Seuss story in rhythm, content, and form.) But it combines the humor with equal amounts of horror. The dreadful experience certainly teaches the old man his lesson: "And he said to himself as he bolted the door,/'I will not wear a similar dress any more,/Any more, any more, any more, never more!' " With this emphatic finality Lear renounces the devil-may-care nonconformity and adventure for adventure's sake that infuse his previous work. He would return to them "never more."

Laughable Lyrics, the volume that contains "The New Vestments," appeared in 1877, the last of Lear's nonsense books to be published during his lifetime. Its contents display a maturity befitting a last work. The altered tone may reflect the settled, travel-weary poet, who has learned that voyages of adventure rarely result in miraculous happiness. Or, given Lear's many-sided perspective on things, it may reflect just another way of looking at situations he had formerly treated lightly or optimistically. One can pair several poems in this volume with counterparts in *Nonsense Songs* and observe illuminating contrasts. In general, *Laughable Lyrics* contains no animated inanimate objects, fewer animals, and more nonsense creatures unique to Lear. The poetic diction is less childish and the poetic structure more complex. The songs in the *Lyrics* do not evoke the world of fairy tale and nursery rhyme as strongly as do those in *Nonsense Songs*. And rather than stress escape from an unsatisfactory existence, they focus on the characters' attempts to compensate for loss or loneliness without simply evading them as the daddy long-legs and the fly had attempted to do. These poems have a distinct Darwinian strain: adapt or perish. Characteristically, though, Lear does not settle decisively on either alternative as preferable. Most of the adaptive mechanisms the characters employ have a touch of the ludicrous and the self-delusive. It is difficult to tell whether Lear approves of them as saving illusions or uses them to ridicule all those rationalizations by which people convince themselves that an absurd planet is the best of all possible worlds.

One poem that raises this question is "The Dong with a Luminous Nose," the only one in the volume that Lear composes as an overt companion piece to a previous verse, "The Jumblies." "The Dong" qualifies the universal happiness achieved in that poem by showing the devastating effect the Jumblies' voyage has had on the Dong, a native of those far off lands they reach in their sieve:

> Long years ago
> The Dong was happy and gay,
> Till he fell in love with a Jumbly Girl
> Who came to those shores one day.[28]

During the Jumblies' sojourn the Dong knows communal as well as romantic love, as he joins in their celebration with its familiar elements of music, dance and moonlight:

> Happily, happily passed those days!
> While the cheerful Jumblies staid;
> They danced in circlets all night long,
> To the plaintive pipe of the lively Dong,
> In moonlight, shine, or shade.

But then the Jumblies sail home. Instead of the triumphal reception the earlier poem describes as resulting from their return, "The Dong" portrays the desolate lover:

> . . . left on the cruel shore
> Gazing—gazing for evermore,—

> Ever keeping his weary eyes on
> That pea-green sail on the far horizon.

The Dong will not accept the loss and resolves to wander over
"valley or plain . . . lake and shore/Till I find my Jumbly Girl
once more!" He stubbornly refuses adaptation, in the form of
resignation to the unalterable. And yet he adapts quite well to the
difficulties of his new role as seeker for his lost love. To facilitate
his night searches, he designs as a lantern a "wondrous Nose"
made from the bark of the Twangum Tree:

> A Nose as strange as a Nose could be!
> Of vast proportions and painted red,
> And tied with cords to the back of his head.
> —In a hollow rounded space it ended
> With a luminous Lamp within suspended,
> All fenced about
> With a bandage stout
> To prevent the wind from blowing it out;—
> And with holes all round to send the light,
> In gleaming rays on the dismal night.

This amazing apparatus, as well as the "plaintive pipe," announces
the Dong's sexual frustration with a crude phallic symbolism that
none of Lear's other long noses begins to approach in obvious-
ness. Although the Dong does not adjust sensibly to his abandonment by his love, he does find a purpose in life and a symbolic
way to express, and perhaps externalize, his grief.

But is the reader to admire the Dong or to laugh at him? The
opening stanzas, which introduce his nightly peregrinations with
an aura of Byronic brooding and Gothic mystery, qualify as some
of the best poetry Lear ever produced:

> When awful darkness and silence reign
> Over the great Gromboolian plain,
> Through the long, long wintry nights;—
> When the angry breakers roar
> And they beat on the rocky shore;—

When Storm-clouds brood on the towering heights
Of the Hills of the Chankly Bore:—

Then, through the vast and gloomy dark,
There moves what seems a fiery spark,
   A lonely spark with silvery rays
   Piercing the coal black night,—
   A Meteor strange and bright:—
Hither and thither the vision strays,
   A single lurid light.
Slowly it wanders,—pauses,—creeps,—
Anon it sparkles,—flashes and leaps;
And ever as onward it gleaming goes
A light on the Bong-tree stem it throws.[29]

Nevertheless one senses a touch of parodic exaggeration in these
lines, particularly in the accumulation of adjectives and the juxtaposed verbs in the sequence from "wanders" to "leaps." As the
Dong transforms himself into this rather ludicrous Wandering
Jew of nonsense land and sets out on his quest, he himself remarks, "What little sense I once possessed/Has quite gone out
of my head!" But since the Dong inhabits a nonsense world,
could this loss of sense not indicate the attainment of a higher
wisdom? Is he an uncompromising Romantic idealist or a love-
sick fool? The poet informs us in the concluding stanza that the
Dong's quest is hopeless: "While ever he seeks, but seeks in
vain/To meet with his Jumbly Girl again." He leaves open the
question of whether his perseverance in a lost cause should be
considered noble or idiotic. Lear perhaps created his nonsense
world in order to avoid answering questions like these.

    He does at least explore the matter further in "The Courtship
of the Yonghy-Bonghy-Bò," which shares with "The Dong"
the theme of love found and then snatched away.[30] While "The
Dong" may express Lear's feelings of rejection and loneliness
symbolically, "The Yonghy-Bonghy-Bò" comes much closer to the
actual details of his life. Commentators agree that the Bò is Lear
himself, Lady Jingly Jones is Gussie Bethell, and the poem is a

fictionalization of their abortive romance.[31] Several other details from Lear's experience find their way into the poem. Noakes believes that the name of the Yonghy-Bonghy-Bò was inspired by a southern Italian muleteer Lear employed during his travels in Calabria who "to Lear's delight . . . finished every incomprehensible sentence with the refrain 'Dighi Doghi Dà.' "[32] The name might equally well derive from a musical evening supplied by some Albanian gypsies while Lear was visiting that country in 1848: "The last performance I can remember to have attended to, appeared to be received as a capo d'opera: each verse ended by spinning itself out into a chain of rapid little Bos, ending in chorus thus: 'Bo, bo-bo-bo, BO!—bo, bobobo, BO!' "[33]

Moreover, throughout the poem the nonsense world and the "real" world come into closer proximity than usual. "The Coast of Coromandel/Where the early pumpkins blow" sounds like a fitting nonsense location, from which one could easily proceed to the Gromboolian plain or the Hills of the Chankly Bore. But in fact it is situated on the Bay of Bengal in southeastern India; Lear had visited this region during his last great excursion in 1873. The Bò is a nonsense creature who also appears in one of the alphabets; Lady Jingly is a human being from England. Because this poem deals with his own experience so closely, Lear sets it in a twilight zone between the worlds of sense and nonsense.

The lonely Yonghy-Bonghy-Bò is materially poor: "Two old chairs, and half a candle,—/One old jug without a handle,—/These were all his worldly goods."[34] With these worldly goods he would gladly endow Lady Jingly. He can in addition offer an abundance of food ("Fish is plentiful and cheap"), Lear's pervasive symbol of caring, and an inexhaustible supply of love: "As the sea, my love is deep!" Although the lady returns his love, the proposal comes too late. She has already bound herself to one of "them": "Handel Jones, Esquire, & Co." Jones's corporate connections suggest money and respectability; his first name may connote the pompous religious orthodoxy Lear despised. (*Handel* also means "trade" or "business" in the language of the Germans the poet detested.) The full name "Handel Jones" also clearly puns with inverse alliteration on the Bò's "old jug without a handle." For the Bò, like Lear himself, does lack a "Handel," an aristocratic name and all the material advantages (and perhaps sexual potency as well) that Jones can bestow upon his wife. However, the relationship between the Joneses appears solely materialistic. He sends Dorking Hens with delight, but does not come to join her on the Coromandel Coast. Nevertheless, Lady Jingly cannot break with loveless convention, and she responds in her husband's manner to her would-be lover: "I can merely be your friend!/—Should my Jones more Dorkings send,/I will give you three, my friend!" She then banishes the Bò from her company, and he responds to his loss, like so many Learian characters—and Lear himself—by running away.

Lear of course has altered the facts somewhat and telescoped the events of his drawn-out romance with Gussie. Unlike Lear, the Bò does propose only to have his love reject him because she is already married. Gussie may have married Adamson Parker because Lear never got around to proposing to her. So the poet is painting himself in a more sympathetic light than the actual circumstances would seem to warrant. He had, however, experienced sister Emma's discouragement of his proposal and Gussie's later marriage as rejections, and the rearrangement of the events in "The Yonghy-Bonghy-Bò" strengthens the poem's fidelity to his emotions. And by including two wretched lovers in the poem, in contrast to a single deserted Dong, Lear also allows himself to express both sides of his conflicting feelings about marriage. When the Bò mounts a turtle, who appears fortuitously like the pig in "The Owl and the Pussy-cat" and the boat in "The Daddy Long-legs and the Fly," he sails away "with a sad primaeval motion," but he can still muster a song. He seems likely to adapt to a solitary existence on "the sunset isles of Boshen." The Bò's reaction may reflect Lear's anxieties that marriage might restrict his freedom.

But the poem concludes with Lady Jingly, who can neither throw off conformity, like one of the eccentrics, in order to follow the Bò, nor resign herself to her former life. Like the Dong, she is trapped in a self-made purgatory, and she sits paralyzed (by guilt?), incapable of even his pitiable attempts to regain happiness:

> From the Coast of Coromandel,
>> Did that Lady never go;
>>> On that heap of stones she mourns
>> For the Yonghy-Bonghy-Bò.
> On that Coast of Coromandel,
> In his jug without a handle
> Still she weeps, and daily moans.

This situation rather strangely reverses that in the "Dong"; for here it is the faithful male lover who sails away and it is the rejecting female who, left on the "cruel shore," laments forever the loss of love. It would, I think, be inconsistent with Lear's personality and his continuing affection for Gussie to see this gloomy portrait of Lady Jingly sobbing over her lost opportunity as a wish-fulfillment punishment of Gussie for having married someone else. By the end of the poem Lady Jingly no longer stands for Augusta Bethell but has turned into an image of Lear's loneliness, reflecting not only his loss of Gussie but all the separations of his life, from Lushington, from Fortescue, from his mother. Because Lady Jingly creates her own predicament by rejecting commitment to love, one suspects that Lear felt himself both victim and cause of all the abandonments he had suffered over the years.

Lady Jingly's fate further comments on the question of adapting to loss that Lear presents so ambiguously in "The Dong." In "The Yonghy-Bonghy-Bò," and perhaps, in retrospect, in the former poem as well, the question of whether one ought to resign oneself to circumstances or defy them becomes moot. Often adaptation depends more on capability than volition. No matter how necessary Lear may have believed adaptability to be, he senses that for many it is simply impossible. Lady Jingly and the Dong, miserable as they are, may therefore be seeing life clearly and seeing it whole. And two other poems in *Laughable Lyrics*, "The

Pobble Who Has No Toes" and "Mr. and Mrs. Discobbolos,"
which portray characters who accept loss cheerfully and make the
best of it, do not add any additional certainty; for in each case
the characters' methods of adapting can be read either as prag-
matically sensible or as blindly self-deluding.

While the two poems that portray a failure to resign oneself
to loss concern an unsuccessful quest for love, the two that depict
acceptance of loss do not involve courtship.[35] They reflect the
settled domestic world of the Sparrows rather than the romantic
wanderings of the owl and the pussy-cat. The plot of "The
Pobble" in fact carefully reverses the pattern of the journey poems.
Like "The New Vestments," it also represents the victory of the
spirit of "them" over the carefree recklessness of the eccentric.
The poem opens in limerick fashion with an exchange between
the Pobble and "they":

> The Pobble who has no toes
>   Had once as many as we;
> When they said, 'Some day you may lose them all,'—
>   He replied,—'Fish fiddle de-dee!'[36]

However, because the first line informs us that the Pobble had
indeed lost his toes, the nonsense reply to "their" meddlesome
solicitousness does not carry the sense of triumph it does in a
limerick such as

> There was an old person of Sestri,
> Who sate himself down in the vestry,
> When they said 'You are wrong!'—he merely said 'Bong!'
> That repulsive old person of Sestri.

The Pobble lives with his Aunt Jobiska, a fussy mother-figure
whom Lear may have drawn on the model of his sister Ann. The
welfare of his toes is her principal concern in life. She doses
him with medicinal "lavender water tinged with pink" because
"The World in general knows/There's nothing so good for a
Pobble's toes!" When she sends him on an errand, to swim

the Bristol Channel to catch fish for her cat, she has him wrap
his nose in scarlet flannel because

> . . . 'No harm
> 'Can come to his toes if his nose is warm;
> 'And it's perfectly known that a Pobble's toes
> 'Are safe,—provided he minds his nose.'

But the Pobble does not mind his nose carefully enough. A porpoise carries away the flannel, and the toes mysteriously disappear:

> And nobody ever knew
> From that dark day to the present,
> Whoso had taken the Pobble's toes,
> In a manner so far from pleasant.
> Whether the shrimps or crawfish gray,
> Or crafty Mermaids stole them away.

"They" must now bring the prostrate Pobble home to "his Aunt
Jobiska's Park." Her reaction to the catastrophe is rather puzzling.
She does not chide the Pobble for his carelessness, or bewail the
loss of his toes, but without batting an eye assures him that
"It's a fact the whole world knows,/That Pobbles are happier
without their toes." While such a statement does not technically
contradict Aunt Jobiska's earlier pronouncements—they had all
concerned the welfare of the toes, not the benefits or drawbacks
of possessing them—it certainly does represent an abrupt about-
face in attitude. Is she a hypocrite, like the fox with the grapes?
Is she determined, like Pangloss, to prove that whatever is is
for the best? Is she simply telling her nephew a consoling lie? Or
is she a fatalist who knows that one must accept the blows of life
and continue on bravely? Again Lear displays an extremely ambivalent attitude toward adaptation to circumstance.

The poem becomes even more ambiguous when one realizes
that although the Pobble takes all the risks and suffers the loss,
the verse concentrates mainly on the reactions of his aunt. Except
for his opening "Fiddle de-dee," he never speaks in the poem.

He is a passive character who constantly has things done to him. Aunt Jobiska "made him drink" the lavender water. She sent him to swim the channel. The porpoise and the undetermined assailant stripped him of flannel and toes without his even being aware he had been attacked. He had to be placed in "a friendly Bark," rowed home, and "carried up." The poet even reports his request for food indirectly, and as "an earnest wish." What defect has rendered this creature so powerless? And why should his life always have revolved around the condition of his toes?

Having examined Lear's works up to this point, one finds the answer fairly obvious, given the intimate connection between nose and toes. The Pobble has been emasculated.[37] The poem deals with a losing struggle to maintain potency, in all senses of the word. Raised in a smothering, effeminate atmosphere, the Pobble is symbolically castrated the moment he sets out into the world to do a man's job. The reverse echoes of "The Owl and the Pussy-cat," the closest thing to a conjugal poem that Lear ever wrote, serve to illustrate the Pobble's incapacity for such affairs. The Pobble goes to sea alone and on a domestic errand in the Bristol Channel, not with a lover and with an exotic land as his destination. His poem contains a "pussy-cat" also, Aunt Jobiska's "Runcible Cat with crimson whiskers"; but the Pobble does not share a feast with it. He must instead provide the food for the "runcible" creature, not enjoy his own food with a "runcible spoon" as do the protagonists of "The Owl and the Pussy-cat." If his function is analogous to that of any creature in the previous poem, it is to that of the pig who must surrender its ring, as the Pobble surrenders his toes. And the pig was at least paid a shilling! The owl and the pussy-cat make their nuptial voyage in a pea-green boat; the porpoise who carries off the flannel is "sea-green."[38] The fowl and the feline row their own boat; the Pobble must be rowed home by "them." While both poems conclude with a meal ("And she made him a feast at his earnest wish/Of eggs and buttercups fried with fish"), one celebrates a wedding and is followed by a dance, while the other provides much-needed nourishment for a weakened traveler. In each case the Pobble's situation provides an impotent variation on a positive action by the two lovers.

One might, therefore, read Aunt Jobiska as a representative of all the women in Lear's life, from his mother, to Ann, to Gussie, and as a focus for all his negative feelings about them. Under a guise of solicitousness and conformity with social wisdom—Mrs. Sparrow springs immediately to mind—women emasculate a man, then expect him to cope with a virile world of "sailors and admirals."[39] And when the experience totally incapacitates him, they blandly cook supper and assure him that he will be much happier as a eunuch. One doubts that Lear consciously composed "The Pobble" to express such hostilities, but they do lurk beneath its surface. Even with the Freudian perspective retained, however, an alternative reading, as is usual in Lear, suggests itself. His sexuality caused Lear so much distress that he may have agreed wholeheartedly with Aunt Jobiska that Pobbles (people?) really are better off without their "toes."

On the other hand, abandoning the sexual symbolism, one can read the poem as another expression of the theme of safe but limiting domesticity that begins with "Mr. and Mrs. Spikky Sparrow" and "The Table and the Chair" and continues in "The New Vestments." All these poems deny the faith that travel can bring transcendent happiness that the journey poems, particularly "The Jumblies," endorse. In "The Pobble," it becomes dangerous to venture outside the door. "Mr. and Mrs. Discobbolos" continues this theme. At the same time it stresses the reduced quality of life that avoidance of danger—one form of adaptation to the precarious nature of Lear's universe—may necessitate. In form the poem returns to the exchange-of-dialogue stanza structure and stanza-ending refrain of the *Nonsense Songs*. Its title suggests that of "Mr. and Mrs. Spikky Sparrow," and, in fact, "Mr. and Mrs. Discobbolos" uses the anxious concern of its title couple for one another's welfare, expressed through conventional circumlocutions and traditional terms of endearment, to parody the cozy married bliss that Lear had portrayed so unconvincingly in "Mr. and Mrs. Spikky Sparrow." Now he sees clearly that cowardice and self-deception often lie at the root of such "happy" domesticity.

Mr. and Mrs. Discobbolos set out one day on a seemingly innocuous sightseeing picnic:

> Mr. and Mrs. Discobbolos
> Climbed to the top of a wall.
> And they sate to watch the sunset sky
> And to hear the Nupiter Piffkin cry
> And the Biscuit Buffalo call.
> They took up a roll and some Camomile tea.[40]

As most Lear characters are when sharing food, they are "as happy as happy could be." But then fear seizes the wife. She imagines that during their descent they might "fall down flumpetty/Just like pieces of stone!" With an equation of good health and proper clothing analogous to that made by Mrs. Sparrow, she inquires of her husband:

> 'What would become of your new green coat?
> 'And might you not break a bone?
> 'It never occurred to me before—
> 'That perhaps we shall never go down any more!'

She then engages in a clever bit of marital blame-passing, inquiring disingenuously of "my own darling Mr. Discobbolos": "What put it into your head/To climb up this wall?"

Her husband cannot dispel her fears, or deny his responsibility for their plight. But after a brief period of embarrassment, during which his ears turn "perfectly pink," he decides that their apparent predicament is actually a blessing in disguise. Just as Aunt Jobiska asserts that Pobbles are happier without their toes, he declares:

> 'But now I believe it is wiser far
> 'To remain for ever just where we are.'

So despite their fear of falling both Discobboloses stand up on the wall and declare in a song that they have stumbled into paradise:

> 'Far away from hurry and strife
> 'Here we will pass the rest of life,
> 'Ding a dong, ding dong, ding!
> 'We want no knives nor forks nor chairs,
> 'No tables nor carpets nor household cares,
> 'From worry of life we've fled—
> 'Oh! W! X! Y! Z!
> 'There is no more trouble ahead,
> 'Sorrow or any such thing—
> 'For Mr. and Mrs. Discobbolos!'

Few efforts at rationalizing away ill fortune could be more complete.

Again the question of how Lear views such adaptability to disaster returns. On the one hand, a passage from a letter to Fortescue shows that Lear sometimes shared the Discobboloses' view that it is better to escape the hurry and strife of earthbound life: "Going up and downstairs worries me, and I think of marrying some domestic henbird and then of building a nest in one of my own olive trees, where I should only descend at remote intervals during the rest of my life."[41] On the other hand, Lear knew that one could not escape life so easily, and he must intend us to see that the Discobboloses have to go through considerable mental gymnastics in order to turn calamity into blessing. And if their contentment at the end of the poem seems to justify the self-deception, Lear typically turns the tables once more by writing in 1879, at Wilkie Collins's request, a second part to the poem that quite literally blows up the complacency of Mr. and Mrs. Discobbolos.

The sequel finds them still on their wall after twenty years. They are happy, healthy, well regarded by their neighbors, and the parents of twelve fine children. But Mrs. Discobbolos becomes

anxious about the children's isolation from normal social life. So
she inquires: "Did it never come into your head/That our lives
must be lived elsewhere,/ Dearest Mr. Discobbolos?"[42] It is a
fatal quesion. Declaring his wife a "runcible goose," Mr. Discobbolos slides down from the wall, digs a trench, fills it with
dynamite and gunpowder, and blows himself and his family "In
thousands of bits to the sky so blue." Does this awful destiny
punish the wife's desire to tamper with an idyllic personal existence for the sake of social conformity; or does it illustrate that
adaptation to ill fortune can become so complete that one refuses
to take advantage of other opportunities when they come along?
(The husband's mission of destruction ironically demonstrates that
the family could have come down safely from the wall at any
time.) Lear is noncommittal:

> And no one was left to have said,
> 'O, W! X! Y! Z!
> 'Has it come into anyone's head
> That the end has happened to all
> Of the whole of the Clan Discobbolos?'

Despite the sadness and the many calamities in the *Nonsense Songs*
and *Laughable Lyrics*, no one dies in any of them except here.
Byrom suggests that by blowing up this family Lear is having
revenge for his unhappy childhood, destroying socially respectable
domesticity and denying that he has lost anything worthwhile in
lacking it as a child or parent: "In this splendidly riotous death
joke there is a great deal of relief. The home that smashed the
child's spirit has itself been smashed. The delusive hopes that
misled the grown-up's spirit have at last been dashed."[43]
     Certainly the poem travesties the cloying, bourgeois family to-
getherness of Mr. and Mrs. Sparrow. Both poems contain a
domestic establishment on a high perch, a nagging wife, and
concern with what society views as proper. But birds at least belong
in trees, if not in fashionable clothes, while "octopod" Discobboloses are only living an illusion of happiness and belonging on
that wall. And once social reality "comes into" Mrs. Discobbolos's

head, her formerly adoring and agreeable husband turns into "terrible Mr. Discobbolos," a suicidal/homicidal maniac, a dynamite-wielding nihilist.

In fact, all of the family's problems materialize only at the instant in which they "come into [someone's] head," a phrase used in seven of the nine choruses. Thus there is irony in the final refrain, in which no one is left to have the realization of the final destruction come into his head. Initially the couple fearlessly climbs the wall until the fears of falling come into Mrs. Discobbolos's head. She assumes that the idea for the excursion was "put into" her husband's head. Likewise, it suddenly comes into his head that they will never get down. Her decision that the children must go into society also comes into her head, and she chides her husband because the idea never came into his. Then the situation turns around, and suddenly Mr. Discobbolos raises the accusing voice: "What has come to your fiddledum head!" However, the idea of blowing up his family does not "come into" his head; he simply acts. Nor does his wife's "We shall presently all be dead" "come into" her head. She simply knows; for now both are going on instinct, not reason. So perhaps what Lear uses his nonsense to attack here is not the bourgeois family per se, but the world of sense to which such families belong. After all, where would the Jumblies have been if it had suddenly come into their heads that their sieve was dangerously full of holes? In most of the *Laughable Lyrics* the defiant spirit of the Jumblies and the limerick protagonists has proved powerless against fate. In "Mr. and Mrs. Discobbolos" Lear can grant that spirit no positive achievements, but he can at least allow it to blow up all those sensible stay-at-homes who fool themselves into believing that, no matter what losses they suffer, they will be happy if they only do what everyone else approves of.

If "Mr. and Mrs. Discobbolos" refutes the domestic conformity of the Sparrows by utterly annihilating it, another poem, "The Pelican Chorus," merely mocks it with sympathetic humor. Once again Lear is taking a basic situation and viewing it from many perspectives. The two verses about bird families share several surface similarities, paramount among them the fact that they both do describe families of birds. Lear carries over from the limericks a disinclination to portray nuclear families of humans and a compensating fondness for portraying familial establishments composed of birds. In addition the pelicans, like the Sparrows, admire fashionable attire, as their detailed description of the "grandly dressed" King of the Cranes demonstrates. Both poems employ couplets and a refrain couched in nonsense bird language, although in the "Pelican Chorus" the annoying "twikky wikky wee" of the Sparrows is replaced by one of Lear's most charming musical effusions:

> Ploffskin, Pluffskin, Pelican jee!
> We think no Birds so happy as we!
> Plumpskin, Ploshkin, Pelican jill!
> We think so then, and we thought so still![44]

However, the domestic milieux of the two poems differ substantially. "Mr. and Mrs. Spikky Sparrow" portrays a comfortable but economy-minded middle-class establishment; the pelicans are king and queen of their kind. And the major event they recollect in flashback in the poem, the "coming out" of their daughter Dell and her subsequent courtship with and marriage to the King of the Cranes, takes place in the midst of the highest of high society. Lear's emotional associations with middle-class domesticity were all negative and intense, so that the attempt to picture the happy sparrow family rings false. But he knew the aristocracy quite well without having any emotional investment in its mores. Therefore he could detach himself to satirize its foibles without malice and depict its joys without envy.

King and Queen Pelican assume their superiority to other birds with the unthinking assurance that so often accompanies birth into a noble station:

> No other Birds so grand we see!
> None but we have feet like fins!
> With lovely leathery throats and chins!
>
> .   .   .   .

> Wing to wing we dance around,—
> Stamping our feet with a flumpy sound,—
> Opening our mouths as Pelicans ought,
> And this is the song we nightly snort.

Through incongruous word choice such as "leathery," "flumpy," and "snort" Lear suggests that such assumptions of superiority are often ludicrous, with little basis in objective fact. The poem also depicts the gala society gatherings where "Thousands of Birds in wondrous flight/. . . ate and drank and danced all night," and the concealed taints of blood: "And a delicate frill to hide his feet,—/(For though no one speaks of it, every one knows,/He has got no webs between his toes!)." No doubt many of Lear's society friends could see themselves underneath the feathers.

While serving as a parody of a fashionable entertainment, Dell's debut represents at the same time still another of those communal feasts, like those that the Dong reflects upon, that the Jumblies celebrate in their sieve and repeat with their friends when they return, that the owl and the pussy-cat partake in after their marriage. All the elements of the Learian epiphany appear: singing and dancing; the sharing of food as a symbol of love ("For the King of the Cranes had won that heart,/With a Crocodile's egg and a large fish-tart"); the color of the crane's "pea-green trowsers"; the shore in the moonlight. But for the first time in one poem Lear combines the happy journey to nonsense land with the portrayal of those whom the travelers leave behind on the cruel shore. "The Pelican Chorus" is both "The Jumblies" and "The Dong," both "The Nutcrackers and the Sugar Tongs" and "Calico Pie." So in the last stanza the tone changes from one of boistrous humor, more characteristic of the *Nonsense Songs*, to the familiar melancholy of *Laughable Lyrics*:

> And far away in the twilight sky,
> We heard them singing a lessening cry,—
> Farther and farther till out of sight,
> And we stood alone in the silent night!

> Often since, in the nights of June,
> We sit on the sand and watch the moon;—
> She has gone to the great Gromboolian plain,
> And we probably never shall meet again!
> Oft, in the long still nights of June,
> We sit on the rocks and watch the moon;—
> —She dwells by the streams of the Chankly Bore,
> And we probably never shall see her more.

The synthesis allows Lear to accommodate his ambivalence about families, love, and society better than in any other single poem. "We probably never shall see her more" echoes "And they never came back to me," but the "probably" cancels out total despair. Unlike the Sparrows, whose children are not ready to leave the nest, the pelican family must split up. Dell flies off to begin her own family, and the king and queen, while "alone in the silent night"—and *silent* is a negatively charged word for Lear—are not really alone. They still have each other and their subjects.

Nevertheless, King and Queen Pelican have been excluded from the world of miracles. They must remain in the real world, on the existing Nile in the actual month of June, while their daughter has entered the timeless nonsense landscape of Gromboolian plain and Chankly Bore. Like the other protagonists in *Laughable Lyrics* they have suffered loss and must reconcile themselves to it. Thus, when they repeat the refrain for the last time, one notices that they "think" no birds as happy as they. Their happiness is not real; they have only convinced themselves that they possess it, just like Aunt Jobiska and Mr. Discobbolos in the first part of his poem. The confused verb tenses of "We think so then, and we thought so still" show the strain of maintaining that no difference exists between genuinely joyful past and forlorn present. Like all successful adapters in the poems, the pelicans delude themselves, but because their loss is the least severe, in this poem their rationalizations sound the least desperate.

Although the mood of the *Nonsense Songs* was generally cheerful, Lear introduced elements of melancholy in "The Daddy

Long-legs and the Fly" and "Calico Pie." Conversely, *Laughable Lyrics* is a generally melancholy volume, but Lear, true to his multi-faceted approach to life, does not fail to include one poem whose happy ending is unqualified. "The Quangle Wangle's Hat" exactly reverses the situation of "Calico Pie," the token unhappy poem in *Nonsense Songs*, and comments as well on those deserted protagonists of *Laughable Lyrics* like the Dong and Lady Jingly Jones. It narrates the reversal of fortune of a lonely being with whom a whole flock of diverse nonsense creatures comes to live. The "me" of "Calico Pie" watches all the creatures of land, sea, and air desert him, and the poem ends with him left alone. The Quangle Wangle, concealed beneath an enormous Beaver Hat as he sits on the top of a Crumpetty Tree, begins in a solitary state:

> 'But the longer I live on this Crumpetty Tree
> 'The plainer than ever it seems to me
> 'That every few people come this way
> 'And that life on the whole is far from gay!'[45]

However, his hat proves as attractive to those seeking shelter as do similar types of headgear in the limericks.[46] After an initial inquiry from Mr. and Mrs. Canary about establishing a home on the hat's 102-foot width

> . . . to the Crumpetty Tree
>   Came the Stork, the Duck, and the Owl;
> The Snail, and the Bumble-Bee,
>   The Frog, and the Fimble Fowl;
> (The Fimble Fowl, with a Corkscrew leg;)
> And all of them said,—'We humbly beg,
> 'We may build our homes on your lovely Hat,—
> Mr. Quangle Wangle, grant us that!
>   Mr. Quangle Wangle Quee!'
>
> And the Golden Grouse came there,
>   And the Pobble who has no toes,—

> And the small Olympian bear,—
>   And the Dong with a luminous nose.
> And the Blue Baboon, who played the flute,—
> And the Orient Calf from the Land of Tute,—
> And the Attery Squash, and the Bisky Bat,—
> All came and built on the lovely Hat
>   Of the Quangle Wangle Quee.[47]

"Calico Pie" is a centrifugal poem, with all elements flying away from a central void; this is a centripetal poem, with all elements converging on the central character. The parade resembles that of the animals in "The New Vestments," but these creatures come to build, not to devour.

The poem ends with the familiar Learian epiphany, now taking place in a blissful present rather than an irrecoverable, remembered past:

> And at night by the light of the Mulberry moon
> They danced to the Flute of the Blue Baboon,
> On the broad green leaves of the Crumpetty Tree,
> And all were as happy as happy could be,
>   With the Quangle Wangle Quee.

With this poem the changing moods associated with the unpredictability of the nonsense universe from the limericks through *Nonsense Songs* and *Laughable Lyrics* comes full circle. If the arbitrary mutability of the world Lear portrays means that one can never be sure of retaining happiness, love, or a place in a community, it also means that isolation and loneliness may vanish just as suddenly as joy. The presence on the hat of two of the more miserable characters from the *Lyrics*, the Pobble and the Dong, as well as others identifiable with the happier *Nonsense Song* protagonists (an owl, a duck, and a married pair of small birds that suggests the Sparrows), underscores the ongoing revolutions of fortune in nonsense land. Lear's poems teach us to guard against complacency, since disaster may lurk around the corner;

they just as firmly teach us to guard against despair because hope may drop out of the sky tomorrow.

"The Quangle Wangle's Hat"

Lear dwells repeatedly on the same problems and examines them from many possible angles, but he gives no final answers. Had he really wished to come to some firm conclusion about adapting to loss and loneliness, he would not have chosen to write the kind of poetry he did. Its ambiguity allows for multiple interpretations and is calculated to prevent any arrival at logical conclusions. Lear did not try to make sense out of life; he regarded such an effort as hopeless. So he made nonsense of it instead.

Two Poetic Autobiographies

Lear wrote two longer poems that never appeared in any of the volumes of verse he published during his lifetime, although he circulated copies of them widely among his friends. Overtly rather than covertly autobiographical, as is characteristic of their author, they view his life from two different perspectives. The first, an untitled collaborative effort with a young friend, Miss Bevan, written in 1878, has become known by its first line, "How pleasant to know Mr. Lear!" It is a descriptive poem, painting a word picture of the appearance, habits, and surroundings of a "crazy old Englishman, oh!" It proceeds through a series of non-sequiturs, using details accurate in themselves but often juxtaposed without logical connectives:

> He reads but he cannot speak Spanish,
> He cannot abide ginger beer.[48]

It also displays the self-deprecating humor about his physical appearance that marks Lear's self-caricatures:

> His mind is concrete and fastidious,
> His nose is remarkably big;
> His visage is more or less hideous,
> His beard it resembles a wig.
>
> His body is perfectly spherical,
> He weareth a runcible hat.

The nonsense songs reveal that these jokes conceal genuine pain, but this verse stays on the external level, with the poet commenting dispassionately upon himself in the third person. The poem thus avoids expressing any of Lear's more disturbing emotions. How seriously can a reader take his description of himself weeping on seashore and hilltop when he immediately follows it with a non-sense menu: "He purchases pancakes and lotion,/And chocolate shrimps from the mill." Although one suspects a self-mocking irony in the phrase "How pleasant," joined in the final two lines to a suggestion of impending death,[49] the poem probably offers a fair approximation of the image Lear presented to the world—a jolly, lovable old eccentric.

The second autobiographical poem, "Incidents in the Life of My Uncle Arly," the last nonsense poem Lear ever wrote, is not a description but a history. It is narrated in the first person, the only poem besides "Calico Pie" to be so, and its melancholy is only partially distanced. True, the poem concerns not "Mr. Lear" but "Uncle Arly," and the first-person speaker is not this figure, but his nephew (or niece). The disguise, however, is paper-thin.

Lear freely acknowledged that the poem was about him; including a draft in a letter to Fortescue in June 1884, he remarked, "I shall send you a few lines just to let you know how your aged friend goes on."[50] As Byrom observes, we soon "spot Lear hiding 'unclearly' in "UncLE ARly,"" and we recognize "the 'Adopty Duncle' of his many 'little folks.' "[51] All the incidents and items mentioned in the poem serve as symbolic nonsense equivalents of events and objects in Lear's life.

"Uncle Arly" begins with a tableau:

> O my agèd Uncle Arly!
> Sitting on a heap of Barley
>   Thro' the silent hours of night,—
>   Close beside a leafy thicket:—
>   On his nose there was a Cricket,—
>   In his hat a Railway-Ticket;—
>   (But his shoes were far too tight.)[52]

By following its use through the songs, one recognizes "silent" as a code word for unhappiness.[53] The leafy thicket may represent the garden at San Remo, or simply the natural scenes that Lear painted. The nose, of course, is the physical feature that stands out. The cricket, most critics agree, represents Lear's nonsense muse.[54] The railway ticket symbolizes the long years spent in wandering. And what about the parenthetical tight shoes? In the letter to Fortescue, which emphasizes this line by adding "Too! too! far too tight!" to it, the distress is quite literal, as Lear follows the stanza with: "By the 15th. May, I was just able to get away from here on my journey of discovery; I was frightfully pulled down by my illness—with swollen feet; and unable to walk."[55] But surely the pinching shoes also suggest the painful limitations of his nature—epilepsy, homosexuality, depression.

The poem then proceeds to relate in flashback how Uncle Arly arrived at the state the first stanza describes. In youth he "squander'd all his goods away" and had to embark on a life of wandering and diverse subsistence jobs:

> Like the ancient Medes and Persians,
> Always by his own exertions
>   He subsisted on those hills;—
> Whiles,—by teaching children spelling,—
> Or at times by merely yelling,—
> Or at intervals by selling
>   Propter's Nicodemus Pills.

Then on a fateful day

> . . . in his morning rambles
> He perceived the moving brambles—
>   Something square and white disclose;—
> 'Twas a First-class Railway-Ticket;
> But, on stooping down to pick it
> Off the ground,—a pea-green Cricket
>   Settled on my uncle's Nose.

Although chronologically out of sequence, since it follows the account of several years of wandering, this stanza must refer to the Knowsley years; for it was at Knowsley that Lear received his "ticket" to travel among "first-class" patrons abroad and at Knowsley that he first began writing nonsense. (The application of his favorite nonsense color, "pea-green," to the cricket reinforces its identification with his poetry.)

Uncle Arly travels for three-and-forty winters—not *years*, since Lear often went home to England in the summers—exactly the amount of time that elapsed from his first leaving England to his settling at San Remo. By this time the shoes are "worn to splinters," although still, paradoxically, "too tight." As the nonsense surely must have, so the cricket provides comfort during the weary and painful travels:

> Never—never more,—oh! never,
> Did that Cricket leave him ever,—
>   Dawn or evening, day or night;—
> Clinging as a constant treasure,—

> Chirping with a cheerious measure,—
> Wholly to my uncle's pleasure,—
> (Though his shoes were far too tight.)

The cricket possibly represents as well the loyal, and constant, companionship Lear had been doomed never to experience with anyone. Perhaps this explains its perching on the phallic nose.

At long last Uncle Arly settles at "Borley-Melling,/Near his old ancestral dwelling." Byrom remarks of these lines that "here Lear seems to prefer fiction to life, for he has Uncle Arly settle not in a nonsense San Remo but in Borley-Melling, a nonsense village near his ancestral home. Lear, of course, had no ancestral home, and those he visited he mostly disliked."[56] I believe, however, that Borley-Melling is indeed a nonsense San Remo and that Lear is using the phrase "ancestral dwelling" with bitter irony. The home he built from the ground up in San Remo and then had to rebuild *was* an ancestral dwelling for a man who felt himself born parentless, who had spent his prime homeless, and who would leave no descendants, only nieces and nephews widely scattered in New Zealand and America. Since Lear was his own sole ancestor and heir, why should he not call the Villa Tennyson an ancestral dwelling? The distance between the commonly assumed meaning of such a term and Lear's private joke expresses succinctly the sense of isolation that dominated his emotional life.

In the first stanza of the poem, Uncle Arly, sitting on his heap of barley with his cricket, resembles Lady Jingly Jones, sitting on her "heap of stones" with her Dorking hens. Doubtless Lear means the image to evoke the same feeling of despair. Unlike Lady Jingly, however, Uncle Arly is allowed by his creator to escape from his misery at last:

> On a little heap of Barley
> Died my agèd uncle Arly,
>   And they buried him one night;—
> Close beside the leafy thicket,—

> There,—his hat and Railway-Ticket;—
> There,—his ever-faithful Cricket;—
> (But his shoes were far too tight.)

Nevertheless, he is ignominiously buried by "they," not "we," as the first-person narration might lead one to assume. And the constricting shoes follow him even to the grave, as do all the few constants of his life.

When "they," the strangers in San Remo, buried Lear, they had carved on the stone an inscription he had left for them: "In Memory of Edward Lear. Landscape painter in many lands. Born at Highgate May 12, 1812. Died at San Remo January 29, 1888. Dear for his many gifts to many souls." It was followed by some lines from Tennyson's poem addressed to Lear, "To E. L., on his Travels in Greece." Had "they" been truly wise, they would have disregarded Lear's instructions and used the last stanza of "Uncle Arly" as his epitaph instead.

Chapter Four

The Other Nonsense

When Lear first began to compose nonsenses, he did so without any thought of publication. Nonsense began as a special language for communication with those he cared for, perhaps as a way to establish intimacy without overt emotional commitment. Only after the success of the original edition of the *Book of Nonsense* did it occur to him that his verses might be works of art rather than simple words and pictures to amuse children and adult friends. Only the nonsense songs seem to have been taken up, relatively late in Lear's life, with a conscious intent of publication from the outset.

When he published his work, he exercised a selectivity that obscures the wide-ranging nature of his nonsense endeavors. As I have noted, for thirty years he considered limericks the only form of nonsense worthy of publication. But during those years he was just as apt to offer his friends alphabets, bizarre menus, pictures with punning captions, or surrealistic narratives as limericks. Lear eventually included examples of these latter varieties of nonsense in the three volumes that he brought out in the 1870s. Because they occupy such a small proportion of his "complete" published nonsense, and because they possess much less appeal than the limericks and longer poems, they appear peripheral to Lear's career. But this impression occurs only because the poet deemphasized them by putting a far smaller ratio of those he produced into print.[1] If one considers all the nonsense Lear composed rather than all that he published, the balance between well-defined nonsense verse forms and miscellaneous, often nonpoetic, nonsense wordplay and storytelling is less lopsided.

Play with language is a central technique of nonsense.[2] It functions primarily to detach words from their conventional usages and remind the reader that they merely symbolize ascribed significances and have no intrinsic meanings at all. Carroll particularly exploits this fact in his books, with the Humpty Dumpty episode in *Through the Looking Glass* being the most famous treatment. Although Lear in the limericks and longer poems also engages in some wordplay—the final adjectives in the limericks, the coined words like "runcible" and "scroobious"—his verse seems distinct from the works of Carroll and other nonsense writers because of its lack of emphasis on that wordplay. But his nonpoetic published nonsense, and, even more so, the nonsense that he created as his special communication in letters to his closest friends reveal that such language games were as integral to his personality as to those of other nonsense artists.

To illutrate the nature of this wordplay and show how it evolved from informal use in communication to formal, publishable nonsense, I will examine the correspondence between Lear and Fortescue and note the relationship of nonsense practices displayed therein to the different groups of "other" nonsense that appear in *Nonsense Songs, More Nonsense,* and *Laughable Lyrics.*

Creative Spelling and the Alphabets

One of Lear's favorite games with words derived not from their meanings but from their sounds and the arbitrariness of English spelling in designating those sounds in one specific way when, phonetically, many combinations of letters would produce the same result. Creative misspellings occur on nearly every page of Lear's letters to "40scue." Many are whimsically unclassifiable, as when he remarks that all his friends are "piers of the Rem, and I am still a dirty Lampskipper" or spells *bosom* "buzzim," *directly* "drekkly," or *politicians* "Polly Titians"; but others belong to identifiable categories of nonsense orthography. When "an" preceded a noun that began with a vowel or *h,* Lear liked to make it conform to the regular use of the article "a" by shifting the *n* to the beginning of the noun. So one reads of "a Nass," "a Noppertunity," "a Notel," "a Noffer," "a Nomlet, "a Nurry," or "a Neasel." He also enjoyed replacing letters with their phonetic equivalents. He gave the underused letter *x* more opportunities by substituting it for *ks, cs, cts,* or *cks* combinations: "monx," "woodcox," "remarx," "waterworx," "fax," "toppix." But, conversely, when *x* occurred naturally in the prefix *ex-* Lear was taken by its phonetic similarity to the word "eggs" and came up with "eggspire" and "eggsibission." Reversals of *f* and *ph* appealed to him as well, as in "phit of coffin," "phame," "Thikphoggs," and "fizzicle."

In addition to substituting soundalike letters for each other, Lear would shift their position within the word and sometimes invert or alter syllables for a comic effect. He invokes that tragic monarch "Mary, Squeen of Cotts" and reports: "I am coming to England fast as I can, having taken a redboom at Hansens 16. Upper Seymour Street, Squortman Pare, and also a rorkwoom or Stew-jew at 15 Stratford Place."[3]

All these eccentrically spelled words are rather like the protagonists of the limericks, recognizable as conventional words/humans, but deviating from the norm in nonsensical ways. Words live for Lear as if they were independent entities. Unlike his coinages, those with variable spellings or transposed letters and syllables are in essence—their sound and signification—of our world; only their clothes—the written combinations of letters—belong to nonsense land.

Lear's interest in the role of each letter in a word is reflected in the many alphabets he wrote and illustrated, sometimes using rhyme, sometimes not. He published only six, three in *Nonsense Songs,* a pseudoalphabet, "Twenty-Six Nonsense Rhymes and Pictures," in *More Nonsense,* and two in *Laughable Lyrics.* Each presents all the letters in a specific verse format and typographical arrangement, headed by a drawing of the object or animal for which the letter stands. The first and third alphabet in *Nonsense Songs* share the same format but use different items as examples, with the exception of the letter X, which is represented in both (and in all but one of the published alphabets) by King Xerxes. The others vary in form but frequently use the same examples, with fish for F, urn for U, yew for Y, and zinc for Z being the most often repeated. As in his other works, Lear seems less interested in letting his imagination expand•than in examining a limited set of ideas from many perspectives. So the variations in approach among the alphabets accompany a certain number of constants.

First Lear assumes that the letter becomes the thing that it illustrates rather than simply representing it. Therefore all but the pseudoalphabet begin "A was an . . ." or "A was once an. . . ." By not using the present tense in these openings, Lear also suggests that a letter can be embodied by many things—as indeed it can— and that he is citing only one of a multitude of incarnations. The notion, very strong in the major poems, that a fish's primary function is to be cooked for supper prevails four of the five times that F is a fish. In general the interest in delineating the characteristics of each representative item reflects concerns similar to those of the limericks: to state that something exists, to describe it, and then to apostrophize it.

Although entitled "Nonsense Alphabets," the three series in *Nonsense Songs* are difficult to perceive as nonsense. The drawings are not stylized or in conflict with the text, the verse describes ordinary animals and things, and the traits ascribed to them are those that they display in real life. In the first series each entry begins with a capital letter with a picture placed underneath. Four lines of verse follow. Beneath this quatrain comes the lower-case form of the letter, followed by Lear's favorite form of punctuation, the exclamation mark. Beneath this letter is a brief exclamation in response to the preceding information.   (See opposite page.) A majority of the verses repeat the final word of the first line in the last (again like the limericks) and rhyme lines two and four of the quatrain while lines one and three are unrhymed. But Lear ten times varies the pattern by making the quatrain into two rhymed couplets. Four times, when the rhyme scheme is of the more

D

D was a duck
With spots on his back,
Who lived in the water,
And always said " Quack! "

d

Dear little duck!

prevalent type, the last word in the final line repeats the last word of the penultimate line rather than of the first. And once, in the entry for S, the endings of the second and last lines match. There is no apparent significance to these variations, but their occurrence shows Lear once again playing with fixed forms in order to illustrate the danger of trusting to any certainty in a changeable world.

The third alphabet in *Nonsense Songs* reprises this format with *ant* becoming *ape* all the way down the line, to *zinc* becoming *zebra*. Although Xerxes is still X, he is notable for his large multi-colored turban rather than another kind of "fashion": "of fury and passion." Its verse form is more standard, sometimes varying the position of the line-ending words that the final exclamation repeats but never departing from the *a/b/c/b* rhyme scheme. Both these alphabets are of the standard children's primer variety, straightforwardly descriptive of the thing the letter stands for; they have little that is distinctively Learian about them.

The middle alphabet in *Nonsense Songs* is somewhat more playful. It foregoes description for a rhyming game that attaches the suffix -y to the illustrative word, to two rhyming adjectives that follow it, then to a two word phrase or pair of adjectives. As in the limericks, the adjectives may either have a logical association with the designated noun ("caky, baky, maky," "owly, prowly, howly") or a nonsensical one ("goosy, moosy, boosey," "henny, chenny, tenny"). The entry ends with an apostrophe to the animal or object:

b

B was once a little bear,
　　Beary,
　　Wary,
　　Hairy,
　　Beary,
　Taky cary,
　Little bear!

This form varies when it takes two or more words to designate the representative item. Then the "little" is eliminated and the last line merely repeats the designating phrase: "apple pie!" "jar of jam!"

"great King Xerxes!" "piece of zinc!" And it varies one more time in the entry "W was once a whale." Although able to conceive of a "little" bear, Lear must insist on a "mighty" whale.

While this alphabet uses word play of the kind geared to the tastes of very young children, it does reveal Lear's interest in the intersections and divergences of sound and meaning as well as the rhyming and repetition common to nursery rhymes. It also contains the kind of wordplay he would use for the "bird talk" in "Mr. and Mrs. Spikky Sparrow" and "The Pelican Chorus."

The one pseudoalphabet in *More Nonsense* much more resembles the limericks that accompany it in that volume than it does the three preceding conventional alphabets. It qualifies as an alphabet in the sense that its "Twenty-Six Nonsense Rhymes and Pictures" describe various animals and persons, the first letters of whose names correspond to each of the letters of the alphabet. But Lear does not arrange the entries totally in alphabetical order; the Umbrageous Umbrella-maker, for example, shares a page with the obsequious Ornamental Ostrich. Nor is the illustrated letter made to stand out through isolating it typographically or using an "A was an . . ." introducing line. Lear stresses it instead through alliteration, ranging from the restrained "Bountiful Beetle" to the tour de force of "The Visibly Vicious Vulture,/who wrote some Verses to a Veal-cutlet in a/Volume bound in Vellum."[5] However, he sometimes clouds the issue by alliterating additional letters not associated with the primary example, as in "The Inventive Indian,/who caught a Remarkable Rabbit in a/Stupendous Silver Spoon."

While the "Nonsense Alphabets" make good learning aids but dubious nonsense, the "Nonsense Rhymes and Pictures" make marvelous nonsense even if their instructional value as alphabets is compromised. They are the only illustrated letter sequence that seems to have been composed in nonsense land. Incongruities abound, beginning with the title "nonsense rhymes," for although the captions accompanying the pictures are arranged in three verse lines, a shorter first and third and a longer middle one, none of the entries contains a single rhyme.[6] The series shows Lear's familiar preoccupations with describing birds in human clothing and accessories and with describing creatures' odd dietary habits. The information that many of the captions provide would be exactly sufficient for crafting a limerick, and the pictorial style also resembles that of the limericks:

"The Perpendicular Polly"

The Perpendicular Purple Polly,
who read the Newspaper and ate Parsnip Pie
with his Spectacles.[7]

Nonsense words, places, and characters from the longer poems occur here as well. There is a Runcible Raven, a Fizzgiggious Fish, a Scroobious Snake, and a Dolomphious Duck who catches her supper in a runcible spoon. The Zigzag Zealous Zebra carries some monkey passengers to Jellibolee, and the illustrative character for Y is none other than the Yonghy-Bonghy-Bò himself.

The final two alphabets, published in *Laughable Lyrics,* are less nonsensical than this, but they do contain more imaginative features than the pure primer variety in *Nonsense Songs.* The first is structured similarly to the two parallel series in that volume, with a quatrain beginning "A was an . . ." and rhyming *a b a b* or *a b c b,* although the final exclamation is missing. But Lear connects the separate entries by having all of them refer in some way to "Papa," particularly (and typically) in regard to the things he eats or wears:

> F was a little Fish.
>   Cook in the river took it,
> Papa said, 'Cook! Cook! bring a dish!
>   And, Cook! be quick and cook it!'

> H was Papa's new Hat;
>   He wore it on his head;
> Outside it was completely black,
>   But inside it was red.[8]

Because it stresses the paternal role, this alphabet also contains several encouragements to good behavior. S is the "thumping Stick" Papa uses to punish "extremely wicked boys," Y is a kicking, screaming youth whose conduct is "abominably bad," and V is a villain who steals a piece of beef. The reader of all the alphabets begins to wonder how King Xerxes will be worked into this scenario, but Lear is equal to the occasion:

> X was King Xerxes, whom
>   Papa much wished to know;
> But this he could not do, because
>   Xerxes died long ago.

Xerxes, however, cannot fit into Lear's final, nonillustrated alphabet. This series of long rhymed couplets makes each letter a character in a story involving an accident and the numerous proposals of remedies for the hurt:

> A   tumbled down, and hurt his Arm, against a bit of wood.
> B   said, 'My Boy, O! do not cry; it cannot do you good!'
> C   said, 'A Cup of Coffee hot can't do you any harm.'
> D   said, 'A Doctor should be fetched, and he would cure the arm.'[9]

and so forth.

Each letter in turn offers the thing it represents as a cure. Most of the cures are edible or drinkable, but Lear also explores the healing powers of Poetry, Song, and music (as played on V's Violin) and the antics of animal companions such as a Kangaroo, Owl, Quail, or Rats "fastened by their tail." The comfortable predictability of the series abruptly ends, however, when Z says, "Here is a box of Zinc! Get in, my little master!/We'll shut you up! We'll nail you down! We will my little master!/We think we've all heard quite enough of this your sad disaster!" One would expect such cruel impatience from one of "them," but in these miscellaneous works Lear as poetic voice frequently indulges in it as long as the characters are so abstracted that their pain exists only in words and does not touch the emotions, so that cruelty is only a joke.

Puns, Botanies and the Wordplay Poems

Lear's experimentation with the spellings and arrangement of syllables of words in his letters is only the first level of his habitual wordplay. He toys not only with the sound of words versus their conventional typographical appearance but with disparities between sound and meaning as manifested in puns. Lear's fondness for punning jokes in private conversation was notorious and often exasperated his acquaintances. The letters contain numerous punning riddles:

What saint should be the patron of Malta?
Saint Sea-bastian. And why are the kisses of mermaids pleasant
    at breakfast?
Because they are a kind of Water Ca-resses.[10]

He also liked to take one word and base free-associating fantasies on it, as in the following disquisition on a "dry" neighborhood:

I never was in so dry a place in all my life. When the little children cry, they cry dust and not tears. There is some water in the sea, but not much: all the wetnurses cease to be so immediately on arriving:—Dryden is the only book read:—the neighbourhood abounds with Dryads and Hammerdryads: and weterinary surgeons are quite unknown.[11]

Or consider his conjugation of *Archipelago*: "But whether I stop here to draw figure, or whether I go to Apulia & Calabria, or whether I Archipela go (V. A. Archipelago, P. Archipelawent, P. P. Archipelagone). . . ."[12]

When he had exhausted all the variations he could turn existing words to, Lear could always invent his own. The nonsense coinages like "scroobious" and "runcible" that appear in the limericks and songs represent only a tiny fraction of Lear's invented words. In general these words are pseudo-Greek[13] or Latinate adjectives that Lear uses to express feelings that real words cannot express; usually there is a tongue-in-cheek acknowledgment of the exaggerated grandeur the impressive but meaningless arrays of syllables give to his emotions. Thus he classifies a projected painting of Bassae with many more "mompophlious matters," broaches a delicate inquiry about patronage for his gallery with a "quapsfillious question," and calls the coast of Malta "pomskizillious and gromphibberous, being as no words can describe its magnificence."[14]

These coinages often reveal with particular clarity that Lear used nonsense to enable him to communicate matters that might have been too painful or embarrassing to report in plain English. In addition, just as the creative spellings show Lear's ability to conceive of individual letters as having a life of their own, the puns and coinages show his parallel conception of words having an existence beyond any attached meaning.

In the published nonsense Lear combines puns and coinages, along with the pictorial side of his talent, most delightfully in the "Nonsense Botany." He published only three botanies, one each in *Nonsense Songs, More Nonsense*, and *Laughable Lyrics*, with the first two containing a dozen entries and the last eight. The idea for them probably originated in Lear's work as a natural history

illustrator. Each entry consists of a large picture of a nonsense
plant with its "scientific" name printed underneath:

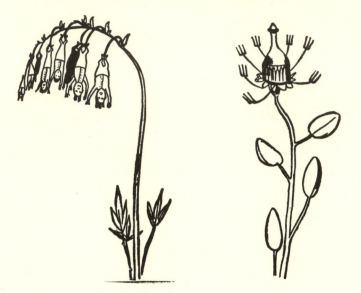

"Manypeeplia Upsidownia"   *"Bottlephorkia Spoonifolia"*[15]

The punning works on several levels here. First of all, Lear is
mocking the pretentiousness of the long Greek or Latin names
for common plants by hiding the names of mundane creatures
and objects within a framework of classical-looking spelling and
word endings. As one Victorian reviewer observed, the botanies
"make our rather artificial and grandiloquent science see the absurd
side of its own pedantry."[16]

The relationship between caption and picture further enhances
the satire. One might glance over names like Phattfacia Stupenda,
Baccopipia Gracilis, or Minspysia Deliciosa, without sounding them
out, and accept them as actual scientific designations. The delight
comes from recognizing their linkage to a huge, fat face on a sun-
flower stalk, to a graceful long-stemmed tobacco pipe extending up

from grassy foliage, to a plate full of delicious mince pies resting on a lily pad. The pictures add still another level of parody in that their various shapes and outlines are those of real plants.

As in his use of nonsense words in the letters, the botanies demonstrate for Lear how easily words can be detached from meaning. To the layman, genuine botanical labels have no intrinsic significance, and it is so refreshing to find in Lear a botany in which a plant labeled "Manypeeplia Upsidownia" is indeed nothing more than a long stem from which many quite contented-looking people hang upside down.

Puns and wordplay become the basis for several extended verse treatments in Lear's last volume of nonsense, *Laughable Lyrics*.[17] Although it fits thematically with the songs, the story of the "New Vestments," discussed in the previous chapter, perhaps belongs in this group as well because of its casual cruelty and its delight in piling up lists of descriptive details. But "The Two Old Bachelors," "The Cummerbund," and "The Akond of Swat" definitely lack the sympathy for their characters that the nonsense songs display. They aim purely at humor, and they base that humor on confusions about the meanings of words.

The joke in "The Two Old Bachelors" derives from a pun on the word *sage*. The title pair live a threadbare existence in one house, and as the poem opens their having "caught" a muffin and a mouse is the only thing to prevent them from going without dinner and therefore losing "our teeth and eyelashes and keep on growing thinner." Whatever sympathy their initial plight might generate disappears when they stubbornly refuse to cook the mouse until they can obtain some sage and onion to make a proper stuffing for it. They borrow an onion, but no sage is to be found. Then "some one"—no doubt a relative of "they"—suggests that since on the "purpledicular" crags to the north there abides

> . . . an ancient Sage,—
> An earnest Man, who reads all day a most perplexing page
> [they should]
> Climb up, and seize him by the toes!—all studious as he sits,—

And pull him down,—and chop him into endless little bits!
Then mix him with your Onion, (cut up likewise into Scraps,)—
When your Stuffin' will be ready—and very good: perhaps.[18]

The thought of cannibalism does not deter the men, for they climb
the crags without "loss of time"[19] and announce to the wise man:
"You earnest Sage! . . . your book you've read enough in!—/We
wish to chop you into bits to mix you into Stuffin'!"

But wisdom easily overpowers gluttony—one of Lear's favorite
morals. The Sage aims his book at the interlopers' heads and sends
them rolling "promiscuous down" the mountain. A further punishment awaits when they land at their door and discover "The
Mouse had fled;—and, previously, had eaten up the Muffin." A
typically Learian resolution follows as they leave their home "in
silence by the once convivial door" and are "never heard of more."
Yet the poem, despite its Learian elements, as a sardonic moral
fable resembles one of W. S. Gilbert's Bab Ballads more than
the gentler majority of Lear's longer poems. Because the *sage-Sage*
confusion is the poem's central point, the poet shows no compunc-
tion in handling its foolish protagonists much more roughly than
he had, for example, the Table and the Chair.

Cruelty and violence also figure prominently in the two other
word play poems, which both grew out of Lear's journey to India.
"The Cummerbund," first published in the *Times of India,* Bombay,
in July 1874, uses a number of Indian words in ways that seem to
fit the poem's syntax but have no correlation with their actual
meanings:

> She sate upon her Dobie,
>   To watch the Evening Star,
> And all the Punkahs as they passed,
>   Cried, 'My! how fair you are!'
> Around her bower, with quivering leaves,
>   The tall Kamsahmahs grew,
> And Kitmugars in wild festoons
>   Hung down from Tchokis blue.[20]

The title refers to that wide sash whose Indian name has now
become a part of the English vocabulary, but in the poem the
Cummerbund is an angry monster with open jaws who "swollows"
the Dobie-sitting heroine, leaving not even "a bone respectfully
to bury." The last verse warns:

> Beware, ye Fair! Ye Fair, beware!
>   Nor sit out late at night,—
> Lest horrid Cummerbunds should come,
>   And swollow you outright.

Except for his use of actual words in an unfamiliar tongue rather
than "portmanteau" coinages, Lear's technique and subject matter
here are almost identical to those of Lewis Carroll in "Jabber-
wocky" (1872); and the similarities between the two poems
indicate that Carroll's verse must have influenced Lear, at least on
this one occasion.

"The Cummerbund" is in the nature of a private joke for an
audience that knows the true meanings of the exotic words. Like
the botanies it shows just how easily we accept nonsense as sense
if it is presented in a verbally camouflaged form. The uninitiated
will assume that Kamsamahs are plants because they grow tall
and have quivering leaves, that "silvery Goreewallahs" that fly "In
silence, side by side" are birds, when in reality the nouns mean
nothing of the sort: a goreewallah (g'horywallah) is a coachman
and a Khamsamah a kitchen steward.

Another playful Eastern poem, which Lear began circulating
among friends in the fall of 1873, ponders the nature of a mysterious Indian potentate, the Ahkond of Swat ("Akond" in the
published version). Lear told Fortescue that he had penned the
"ridiculous effusion" in response to a friend who, seeing the name
in the papers, wrote to ask "who or what is he?" The poem consists of an opening question, "Who, or why, or which, or *what,* Is
the Akond of SWAT?" followed by twenty-two different inter-
rogative couplets, the sense of whose last line is completed by a
phrase ending in a monosyllable that rhymes with the "Swat" in

the ruler's name, which is repeated beneath each couplet, e.g.:

> Does he sing or whistle, jabber or talk,
> And when riding abroad does he gallop or walk, or TROT,
>   The Akond of Swat?[21]

Many probable and improbable speculations ensue, in no particular logical order, in much the same way as Lear lists the details about himself in "How Pleasant to Know Mr. Lear!": "Is he wise or foolish, young or old?/Does he drink his soup and his coffee cold, or HOT," "Does he teach his subjects to roast and bake?/Does he sail about on an inland lake, in a YACHT." The poet even sneaks in a reference to his friend Tennyson: "Does he like to lie on his back in a boat/Like the lady who lived in that isle remote, SHALLOTT." Lear emphasized to Fortescue that "The effective way to read the Ahkond of Swat is to go quickly through the two verse lines, and then make a loud and positive long stretch on the monosyllable—hot, trot, etc: etc:",[22] so it is obvious that sound, not sense, is of primary importance to the poem.

The content of the poem does, however, link it to the other nonsense, once again especially to the limericks. Lear's detailed musings over the many possible diets, habits, wardrobes, and relations with his subjects that the Akond might have could very well represent a written version of Lear's thought processes as he chose which set of facts to present about a limerick protagonist. He simply does not make the decision here. Thus, instead of arriving at "There was an Akond of Swat/Who . . . ," he concludes with a statement, but not an answer to the original question: "Some one, or nobody, knows I wot/Who or which or why or what Is the Akond of Swat!"

The casual cruelty of the limericks and the other "language" poems also appears. After asking whether the people "like him extremely well?/Or do they, whenever they can, rebel, or PLOT," Lear muses on whether he punishes captured rebels, "either young or old," by having them "chopped in pieces or hung, or *shot*." The poet also wonders if the subjects garotte in the park "when days are dark" and whether the Akond beats his wife with a gold-topped pipe if she lets the gooseberries become overripe. But since perpetrators and victims of all this violence are purely hypothetical, since the only reality contained in the poem is an enigmatic title spotted in the newspaper (no illustration accompanies the verse to suggest the Akond's appearance), the violence has even less impact than that in the limericks. Their tone also serves to distance pain but hardly as thoroughly as Lear accomplishes in this rhyming game and his other wordplay poems.

Lear's Prose Nonsense

Such joking about pain and death, coupled with wordplay, is common to Victorian nonsense humor in general, such as that by Thomas Hood, W. S. Gilbert, and, of course, Lewis Carroll.[23] But Lear differs from Carroll in that his nonsense is overwhelmingly poetic or pictorial, while Carroll in the Alice books inserts the occasional poem into a prose narrative. One might make a case for viewing the letters, since they contain so much that is nonsensical, as Lear in Wonderland, but he rarely published genuine prose nonsense. That prose nonsense he did publish should not be overlooked. It follows the pattern of the rest of the miscellaneous nonsense by indulging in puns and the detachment of words from their meanings and in using these techniques to neutralize the emotional impact of tales of pain and death.

One can observe how a single pun could germinate into a complex narrative by tracing the history of the "Phoca Privata" in Lear's letters to Fortescue. The phrase is the Latin version of "Privy Seal," which cabinet post Fortescue, now Lord Carlingford, had assumed in April 1881. Lear immediately seized upon the alternate meaning of *seal* as an aquatic mammal with flippers, and he closed his congratulatory letter of April 14 with a drawing of that animal and the caption "Ye great seal" written beneath it. "Privy Seal" has also become "Phoca Privata" in this letter. The difficulties of caring for and feeding the Phoca and of providing it accommodations should Carlingford visit San Remo run ever more elaborately as a strain throughout the correspondence as long as Fortescue held the office. In March 1882 Lear confessed, "I have never had a clear idea of what the Privy Seal's work really is: and my last notion is that you have continually to superintend seal catching all round the Scotch and English coasts, in order to secure a Government monopoly of seal skin and seal calves."[24] He also appended a description—in Italian—of the progression of the Lord Guardian of the Seal and his charge through the Royal Court that, translated, reads in part as follows:

One cannot well describe the motion of this enormous animal, as Italian is lacking in words that adequately translate 'Wallop,' or 'Flump,' verbs that well suit its motion, but that are unknown to us Italians. Many ladies are a good deal frightened the first time that they see the Great Seal, but they are strictly forbidden to scream. When it has been all round the Gallery, this amiable beast withdraws again with a Wallop-flump, with the Lord Guardian;—and before retiring, the latter gives the Seal more than 37 pounds of macaroni, 18 bottles of Champagne, 2 beefsteaks, and a ball of scarlet worsted,—all of which are brought by 10 servants in livery.[25]

Lear later concocted a newspaper report, also in Italian, about the Phoca's escape and arrival on the San Remo beach, to the consternation of local officials. And when Fortescue resigned the post in the fall of 1883, Lear wrote: "You had better keep President of the Council if so be you ain't Privy Seal also. That creature's life is a dreary mystery to me; but I have already offered you the use of my large cistern if you will send him out.—My two Suliots should take good care of him."[26]

The two stories that Lear included in the *Nonsense Songs* volume are similarly tongue-in-cheek but are aimed specifically at children. Both are tales of adventure about youngsters setting out from home to see new and exciting places. But one, "The History of the Seven Families of the Lake Pipple-Popple," contains a cautionary moral about gluttonous and selfish behavior while the other, "The Story of the Four Little Children Who Went Round the World," describes the preoccupation with food and occasionally vicious actions of its young heroes without overt condemnation. The pairing of the two is typical of Lear's double perspective throughout his works.

"The Four Little Children" has links to the first series of nonsense songs that accompany it in the volume. Its protagonists, Violet, Slingsby, Guy, and Lionel,[27] feel a compulsion to see the world and obtain a large boat for circumnavigatory purposes. They have a cat for a steersman and as cook "an elderly Quangle-Wangle," who at tea time requires a large kettle that at bedtime converts into sleeping quarters. Although Lear would not give the Quangle-Wangle his own published poem until *Laughable Lyrics,* the other details suggest the journeys in both "The Owl and the Pussy-cat" and "The Jumblies."

At the outset the voyage is only marginally nonsensical. They feed on fish, a very "natural" food in Lear's scheme of things. And when Violet attempts to churn salt water "in the hope that it would turn into butter," we learn that it "seldom, if ever did."[28] But as soon as the party sights "an island made of water quite surrounded by earth," the narrative becomes surrealistically incredible. And we notice that the travelers generally seem more interested in gathering provisions for the next leg of the trip than in observing the geography and natives they supposedly undertook the journey in order to see. Lear employs two standard nonsense techniques to heighten the outrageousness of his tale: precise description and enumeration of impossible things and events; and the use of words whose normal definitions negate the meaning that their syntax implies. Both techniques had of course occurred in the letters and in the other nonsense, but they are more prominent here than in any other of Lear's nonsense forms.

Lear's descriptions stress how many, how big, and what color. The numbers tend to be large. The first stop provides the travelers with "two thousand veal-cutlets and a million of chocolate drops," initially observed from atop "a single tree, 503 feet high." They next encounter "sixty-five great red parrots with blue tails" from whom Violet obtains 260 tail feathers. Other enumerated creatures and objects include "oranges . . . by millions and millions," "a countless multitude of white mice with red eyes," "a large number of Crabs and Crawfish—perhaps six or seven hundred," and "fifty-five-thousand-million-hundred-billion bits." (The journey, by contrast, is accomplished in "less than eighteen weeks.")

The wordplay is even more in evidence. Lear pairs contradictory nouns in phrases such as "utmost delight and apathy," "mingled affection and disgust," and "joy tempered with contempt." He plays with inappropriate adjectives in phrases such as "accurately cutaneous inspection," "softly in a loud voice," and "superincumbent confidential cucumbers." Supposedly positive reactions are expressed through the names of diseases. The sight of the huge "Co-operative Cauliflower" gives the children "a strong sense of underdeveloped asthma and a great appetite." A testimonial is subscribed as "an earnest token of their sincere and grateful infection."

All this subversion of words from their conventional usages complements the implicit moral tale the story contains and Lear's subversion of its expected outcome. As in so many other Learian works, food serves as a moral barometer. The children begin as respectful gleaners of what nature has to offer and step by step become predators in a competitive struggle for food that finally leads them to kill when neither food nor self-protection is at issue. When the children arrive at their first shore, they spend a week in the high tree to make sure that the island is uninhabited before helping themselves to the veal-cutlets and chocolate drops. Portents of aggression appear at the next stop, however, when the cat and Quangle-Wangle bite off the tail feathers of the sixty-five parrots. Although Violet "reproved them both severely," she cannot resist decorating her bonnet with the detached feathers. Next the travelers are stranded in a narrow waterway packed with ready-cooked soles upon which they feed for six months. But to assuage their consciences they knit woolen frocks for and administer opium drops to the "few fishes who remained uneaten" and have complained of the cold.

Then their luck in finding food changes. While they are picking the fruit from giant orange trees, a windstorm comes up and sends the oranges pelting down on them. Although bruised, they at least have the oranges to eat. But at their next port of call they do not receive this consolation. They encounter the multitude of mice eating from a giant bowl of custard pudding. When Guy asks the mice for a share of the pudding, they give him only half a walnut shell full, and that diluted with water. He correctly reprimands them for their stinginess only to have "all the Mice turn . . . round at once, and sneeze . . . at him in an appalling and vindictive manner, (and it is impossible to imagine a more scroobious and unpleasant sound than that caused by the simultaneous sneezing of many millions of angry Mice)." Guy then abandons his polite, morally correct attitude and pays the mice back in kind by throwing his cap into the middle of the custard and spoiling it.

The next episode marks the moral pivot of the tale. The children come to a land inhabited by beautiful blue bottle flies living in the "most copious and rural harmony" and in "perfect and abject happiness." The land is a magic one where the party can turn pebbles and hot water into tea by having the Quangle-Wangle play accordion tunes over them. The night they spend with the flies has most of the elements of a Learian epiphany, and the children years later "looked back to that evening as one of the happiest in all their lives." Perhaps to mask the deep emotions that such transient but blissful experiences always evoke in him, Lear describes the scene through a nonsense parody of purple-prose descriptive passages, highlighted by alliteration:

At this time, an elderly Fly said it was the hour for the Evening-song to be sung; and on a signal being given all the Blue-Bottle-Flies began to buzz at once in a sumptuous and sonorous manner, the melodious and mucilaginous sounds echoing all over the waters, and resounding across the tumultuous tops of the transitory Titmice upon the intervening and verdant mountains, with a serene and sickly suavity only known to the truly virtuous. The Moon was shining slobaciously from the star-bespringled sky, while her light irrigated the smooth and shiny sides and wings and backs of the Blue-Bottle-Flies with a peculiar and trivial splendour, while all nature cheerfully responded to the cerulean and conspicuous circumstances.

But then they must leave "that happy shore for ever."

Like many Lear characters made joyful and then abandoned on the cruel shore, the flies can be heard sobbing for hours. The children are also supposedly "overcome by their feelings," but they respond to the painful emotions by instantly falling asleep. Their sensitivity and possibilities for forming positive personal relationships will decrease as the remainder of the journey proceeds. The dried figs the flies give them as one of their departure gifts represent the last exchange of food they have with anyone. They do at their next stop help some friendly and grateful crabs make worsted mittens for themselves, but the next-met Co-operative Cauliflower is too large and remote for any kind of contact save awed observation. Next they sail under a cliff from which "a particularly odious little boy" heaves a pumpkin at their boat and upsets it. However, the Quangle-Wangle gets revenge by filling the pumpkin with lucifer-matches and throwing it back so that "the Pumpkin exploded surreptitiously into a thousand bits, whereon the rocks instantly took fire, and the odious little boy became unpleasantly hotter and hotter and hotter, till his knickerbockers were turned quite green, and his nose was burned off." They next find some Mulberry Jam pits guarded by Yellow-nosed Apes who snore with such "violence and sanguinary sound" that the children, no doubt fearing a repetition of the Mouse incident, steal only a small cupful of the jam and hurry back to their boat without addressing the apes at all. Unfortunately they discover that the boat and all their supplies are in the process of being chomped to bits by "an enormous Seeze Pyder."

Forced to complete the trip by land, they seize an elderly rhinoceros that is passing by and climb upon his back. Although their initial provender consists of a woefully inadequate amount of four small beans and three pounds of mashed potatoes, they have developed sufficient predatory instincts to entrap and roast the wildfowl who "alighted on the head of the Rhinoceros for the purpose of gathering the seeds of the rhododendron plants which grew there." Arriving safely home, they repay the rhino for his services in a manner that Lear details in the concluding paragraph of the story: "As for the Rhinoceros, in token of their grateful adherence, they had him killed and stuffed directly, and then set him up outside the door of their father's house as a Diaphanous Door-scraper." This cruel twist to the tale may indicate a desire on Lear's part to mock the goody-goody moralism of conventional children's stories, but it may also display his true feelings about the injustices of life, the view of the arbitrarily hostile Darwinian universe that characterizes *Laughable Lyrics*. He first wrote the story for the children of Gussie's brother in the week that followed Emma Parkyns telling him not to propose to Gussie. Perhaps Lear saw himself as the faithful elderly rhinoceros whom the children of respectable fathers have decided is only fit to serve as a stuffed doorscraper.

The only other prose narrative Lear published, "The Seven Families of the Lake Pipple-Popple," is in its form more typical of a Victorian cautionary tale for children, illustrating the fatal results of greed, quarreling with siblings, and disregarding the advice of parents. In its use of repetitive patterning in structuring the parallel histories of the seven families it conveys the primerlike quality found in the alphabets. It also contains more carnage than all of Lear's other works put together. At the same time, it continues the playfulness with language, particularly through the strings of Greco-Latinate adjectives that do not quite fit their context: ". . . and hit their heads so vividly against its stalk, that the concussion brought on directly an incipient transitional inflammation of their noses, which grew worse and worse and worse till it incidentally killed them all Seven."[29] This wordplay once again removes emotional impact from the suffering and death.

The seven families of parrots, storks, geese, owls, guinea pigs, cats, and fishes all include two parents and seven children. Their lake is located near the city of Tosh—i.e. a nonsense locality—in the land of Gramblamble. Lear first details their habits, with their dietary practices always uppermost in the description: "The Owls anxiously looked after mice, which they caught and made into sago puddings. The Guinea Pigs toddled about the gardens, and ate lettuces and Cheshire cheese." He then reports how each family eventually sends its offspring out to see the world, provided with "eight shillings and some good advice, some chocolate drops, and a small green morocco pocket-book to set down their expenses in." Each set of parents also makes a "parting injunction" which in all but one of the cases involves the children's obtaining of food for themselves and stresses the necessity of dividing all portions equally without quarreling and avoiding harmful types of food.

Of course, as chapters V through XI reveal, the children do precisely what their parents tell them not to do, so that they meet various violent ends while the potential prey in each case goes unscathed. After the deaths of all the children these intended victims gather in a typical Learian celebration "to rejoice over their good fortune":

. . . they danced a hornpipe round all these memorials until they were quite tired: after which they gave a tea-party, and a garden-party, and a ball, and a concert, and then returned to their respective homes full of joy and respect, sympathy, satisfaction, and disgust.

The epilogue, however, adds a bizarre note to this conventional, if sardonic, moral fable. When the parents "became aware by reading in the newspapers, of the calamitous extinction of the whole of their families," they stopped eating, except for taking a last "light supper of brown bread and Jerusalem Artichokes." They subsequently pickle themselves in seven bottles stopped up and sealed with blue sealing wax. Like the stuffed rhinoceros they end as a perpetual display, in the Tosh museum "on the Ninety-eighth table in the Four hundred and twenty-seventh room of the right-hand corridor of the left wing of the Central Quadrangle of that magnificent building," where, if one does not look, Lear informs the reader, "you certainly will not see them." Such joking with death and tragedy once again makes Lear's nonsense prose come closer to the macabre spirit of Hood, Gilbert, and Carroll than do the more famous poems.

Learian Parody

Another frequent ingredient of Victorian comic writing that Lear's most generally read works do not share is parody. Although critics have frequently remarked elements in the songs that resemble themes and metres employed by serious nineteenth century poets, particularly Byron and Tennyson, the verses that contain them qualify more as imitations or passing allusions than full-scale parodies such as the send-ups of Wordsworth, Southey, and Isaac Watts in the songs in Carroll's books. Lear does not intend to criticize the poems he borrows from by transposing them into a nonsense key. He is too busy establishing nonsense land as a place apart from the every day world to have it contain systematically developed satiric referents to that world.

Lear did, however, fiddle with parodies as a diversion; for example, in order to recall the Tennyson verses that his illustrations were to correspond to, he fashioned travesties of them, including one of the poem Tennyson had dedicated to him. Where Tennyson had written:

> Tomohrit, Athos, all things fair,
> > With such a pencil, such a pen,
> > You shadow forth to distant men,
> I read and felt that I was there.

Lear wrote:

> *Tom-Moory* Pathos;—all things bare,—
> > With such a turkey! such a hen!
> > And scrambling forms of distant men,
> O!—ain't you glad you were not there![30]

He also imitated the style of Clough in "Amour de Voyage" in a letter to Fortescue describing his daily doings;[31] and brief parodies of other well-known verses crop up occasionally in the letters. But he never published any sustained verse parody.

Of his published works one might stretch a point to call the two stories parodies of Victorian children's literature or of flowery diction in general, but more overt parodies make up the *"Nonsense Gazette* for August 1870" that appeared in *Nonsense Songs*. An extract from the *Gazette* announces:

Our readers will be interested in the following communications from our valued and learned contributor, Professor Bosh, whose labours in the fields of Culinary and Botanical science, are so well known to all the world. The first three articles richly merit to be added to the Domestic cookery of every family; those which follow, claim the attention of all Botanists.[32]

I have already alluded to the parodic element in the "Nonsense Botany." Of the three "receipts for domestic cookery" the funniest is that for Gosky Patties, although the others, for Amblongus Pie and Crumbobblious Cutlets, employ precisely parallel comic methods. Lear first imitates the detailed lists and quantities of required ingredients that recipes always contain, except that his is incongruous and inedible:

Take a Pig, three or four years of age, and tie him by the off-hind leg to a post. Place 5 pounds of currants, 3 of sugar, 2 pecks of peas, 18 roast chestnuts, a candle, and six bushels of turnips, within his reach; if he eats these, constantly provide him with more.

Then procure some cream, some slices of Cheshire cheese, four quires of foolscap paper, and a packet of black pins.

He then parodies the step-by-step method for preparing a dish, using the warning phrases that cookbooks always employ to convince the cook that the slightest deviation in procedure will result in ruin:

Work the whole into a paste, and spread it out to dry on a sheet of clean brown waterproof linen.

When the paste is perfectly dry, but not before, proceed to beat the Pig violently, with the handle of a large broom. If he squeals, beat him again.

Visit the paste and beat the Pig alternately for some days, and ascertain if at the end of that period the whole is about to turn into Gosky Patties.

Unlike regular recipes, however, Professor Bosh's allows for failure: "If it does not then, it never will; and in that case the Pig may be let loose, and the whole process may be considered as finished." Lear thus pokes fun at the almost mystical element that enters into the gourmet's conception of successful cookery.

With the "Nonsense Cookery" Lear is once again dwelling on food, which as subject matter, symbol, and moral barometer permeates every phase of his writing. Eating is a popular topic in much literature for children, but Lear's use of it is too prevalent and too complex merely to have been the result of generic expectations. From his girth in later years, one assumes that Lear himself enjoyed food. He delighted in concocting nonsense menus for friends, adults as well as children. He writes Fortescue: "Meanwhile, if you come here directly I can give you 3 figs, and 2 bunches of grapes; but if later, I can only offer you 4 small potatoes, some olives, 5 tomatoes, and a lot of castor oil berries. These, if mashed up with some crickets who have spongetaneously come to life in my cellar, may make a novel, if not nice or nutritious Jam or Jelley."[33] While his play with unlikely mixtures of food parallels his playfulness with words, food also, as we have seen, symbolizes deep, genuine emotions in the nonsense songs.

As a whole the letters and the miscellaneous nonsense show Lear using nonsense as play, as a means for examining pain, violence, and death with emotional neutrality. To ignore these works is to see Lear as more idiosyncratic in the context of Victorian nonsense writing than he actually was. Nevertheless, he leaned away from this playfulness in selecting his nonsense for publication; in the songs emotion is quite apparent and there is often no effort to neutralize it. In the limericks Lear maintains a balance between nonsense as play and nonsense as therapy. The epithet "author of 'A Book of Nonsense' " (which contained only limericks) was automatically attached to his name even after he had published three more varied volumes, even after he had died. This seemingly too narrow tag was perhaps more justified than one might first think. The limericks are not his most ambitious or most accomplished poems, but they remain in the end his most representative, combining more of the many facets of his vision of life and sharing some elements with all the other forms his nonsense writing would take.

Chapter Five
Conclusion

I began this volume by remarking that people have become interested in Lear's life because knowing about it helps one to decode the nonsense. In turn, however, many recent critical studies of Lear seem to find the nonsense important primarily because it comments upon the life. I have myself utilized considerable biographical information in my explications of the nonsense, for once one has become familiar with Lear's biography, the parallels between life and art are impossible to ignore. And yet totally biographical readings of the poems fast assume a tautological, solipsistic air. Certainly Lear's life is not so compelling, or so significant, that his nonsense should stay alive merely to illuminate it. Therefore it seems appropriate to conclude this study by examining the influence of Lear's work itself, without reference to its personal significance to him.

Of course, the nonsense first gained its popularity with readers ignorant of Lear's biography, or even of his identity, as his anecdote about the gentleman on the train so succinctly demonstrates. Lear's obituaries offer additional evidence of his obscurity as an author in proportion to the fame of his works. In the *Athenaeum* the writer notes that "His poetic and technical gifts were, however, less remarkable than his infinite humour and keen-edged wit, expressing itself in a hundred quaint ways"; yet he also reports that Lear was born on the Derby estate, a son of one of the lord's agents or tenants.[1] Twenty-two year later this misconception was still current. Philip Hofer discovers it, taken almost verbatim from the *Athenaeum* piece, in the entry on Lear in Bryan's *Dictionary of Painters and Engravers*, published in 1910.[2] The obituary in the *Academy* offers not even speculation about Lear's biography. The brief notice finds him most noteworthy, aside from being the creator of the nonsense, for inspiring the poem that Tennyson dedicated to him, "To E. L., on his Travels in Greece."

Clearly it was the nonsense itself, quite divorced from its author, that captivated Victorian children and adults. Despite the more complex meanings that critical analysis legitimately reveals in the nonsense poems, that analysis should never negate the surface pleasures of the poems that Lear aimed squarely at the tastes of the children who inspired their creation. The nonsense verses, with their distinctive rhythms, refrains and repetitions, personifications, and absurd imaginary creatures, appeal to the same childish fancies as do nursery rhymes; and the frequently anthologized "The Owl and the Pussy-cat" has partially achieved nursery-rhyme status. But the poems do not patronize their young readers. The limericks, particularly, let the child assume a superior position to the bizarre, misbehaving adults they feature. In its original Victorian context all the nonsense provided, as did, more self-consciously, Lewis Carroll's, a healthy change from the predominant vein of children's literature of the time. This literature was at its best drily didactic and at its worst perversely morbid in its exaltation of the suffering of saintly infants. Lear's poems contain moral lessons of their own, against gluttony and intolerance, in favor of sharing, cooperation, and friendships between diverse creatures,[3] but only "they," of all the inhabitants of nonsense land, would espouse the conventional moralism of the traditional Victorian children's tract.

Lear enjoyed the company of bright, personable children, but he did not sentimentalize all children.[4] He originally composed his various nonsenses to respond to the wishes of various individual youngsters; they contain no platitudes about childhood as an abstract condition. In fact few children appear in the nonsense at all, although he assumed that children would be the primary audience for his published nonsense books. Lear truly wrote *for* children, not about them or at them, as so many of his contemporaries did without realizing the distinctions among the three approaches. Along with Lewis Carroll, he has continued to serve as a standard against which whimsical children's fantasies are measured. For example, a *Time* magazine essay commemorating the seventy-fifth birthday of "Dr. Seuss" observes: "His rhythmic verse rivals Lewis Carroll's, and his freestyle drawing recalls the loony sketches of Edward Lear, perhaps because, like those masters of nonsense, he fathered no children except those of his imagination."[5]

Although Lear's work is decidedly nonconventional by Victorian standards of children's literature, it is in many other respects quite typical of its age.[6] The relationship between "they" and the limerick protagonists explores the conflict between individual liberty and the stability of the social organism, a conflict that frequently concerned and perplexed Victorian writers. It represents one of the irresolvable dilemmas of civilization; the vicissitudes of history favor now one, now the other side, but the ideal equilibrium has rarely been reached, or even satisfactorily described.

The difficulty of description appears clearly in Arnold's *Culture and Anarchy* and Mill's *On Liberty*, primary documents in the fight against repressive social conformity. Although Arnold supports spontaneity of thought, his elite collection of best selves who are to form the enlightened state has decidedly authoritarian overtones. Mill preaches total liberty in theory, but his exceptions in the realm of practical applications leave individuality quite severely circumscribed.

In the Victorian era, when society's power over the individual might extend to the protection not only of life and property, but of propriety, majority opinion, and the cheek of the young person, the scale might on first glance have appeared to have tipped too far in the direction of social stability. But the ambiguities of the question increased because the constrictions of the social mechanism were offset by disturbing changes in the view of the universe at large. The random Darwinian cosmos threatened to leave man much more uncomfortably on his own than the most ardent libertarian might wish. Although the debate proceeded vigorously nevertheless, those Victorians who argued the claims of either "strictness of conscience" or "spontaneity of consciousness" invariably had to take the advantages of the opposing side and the disadvantages of their own into consideration. Depending upon the degree of honesty with which they faced these considerations, they became at best self-contradictory, at worst, hypocritical. A totally honest, unqualified advocacy of either the individual or society seems ultimately impossible, but this situation does not preclude a thorough exploration of the ramifications of their conflict. The limericks provided one of the most sensitive Victorian explorations.

"Nonsense, pure and absolute," as Lear practiced it, serves as an excellent medium for dealing with ambiguous questions because its nature rules out any clear, unequivocal statement. It is non-sense, admirably suited to areas in which empirical sense proves elusive. Lear creates with his multifarious universe an art which encompasses the pro and contra of many views without relying on the logical consistency that would force value judgments among them. Lear's universe also expresses the fears that had caused many of his contemporaries to seek safety in Philistinism. As I have noted, in his longer poems the question of adapting for survival to an arbitrary, Darwinian environment surfaces frequently. The overall unpredictability of nonsense land no doubt appeared to many Victorians as a not so fanciful reflection of conditions in their own rapidly changing world.

Subsequent generations have further blurred the seeming distinction between such an "unreal" poetic creation and actual experience. One discovers elements of Lear's work used as commonplaces to illustrate facets of every day life. John Russell Taylor, writing about Alfred Hitchcock's childhood, observes that "if he revealed anything of what he thought and felt, betrayed his emotions to anyone else, THEY (the harsh, rationalistic, disapproving 'they' of Edward Lear's nonsense poems) would somehow come and get him."[7] Bill Manhoff entitles his 1964 comedy play about an unlikely couple—an uptight intellectual and a brassy prostitute—"The Owl and the Pussy-cat." Webster's Dictionary has an entry for "runcible spoon: a sharp-edged fork with three curved prongs" in which the typical derivation of OE, ME, L, or the like is replaced by "coined with an obscure meaning by Edward Lear."[8]

Meanings are often "obscure" in Lear, but his characters none-theless never abandon a search for them amid the frightening lack of certainty in their world. However, Lear's methods of portraying that lack of certainty appealed equally to artists who did wish to create imaginary worlds devoid of meaning. The arbitrary disasters that befall Lear's creatures have a distinctly Kafkaesque ring, and his games with language resemble those employed in surrealist and existentialist literature and in the theatre of the absurd, upon all of which the strong influence of nonsense in general has long been acknowledged. Martin Esslin notes in his *The Theatre of the Absurd,* in a chapter surveying the relationship between nonsense literature and absurdist drama: "As in the Theatre of the Absurd, and indeed, as in the vast world of the human subconscious, poetry and cruelty, spontaneous tenderness and destructiveness, are closely linked in the nonsense universe of Edward Lear."[9]

But whatever their philosophical or artistic school, writers in general have responded with a particular warmth to Lear. Ruskin's praise in the *Pall Mall Magazine* has been echoed in essays on Lear by such eminent twentieth-century British writers—and third- or fourth-generation *Book of Nonsense* readers—as George Orwell, G. K. Chesterton, and Aldous Huxley. Huxley classified Lear as one of the few authors whose works he enjoyed reading over and over:

It is when circumstances combine to prove, with syllogistic cogency, that life is not worth living that I turn to Lear and find comfort and refreshment. I read him and I perceive that it is a good thing to be alive; for I am free, with Lear, to be as inconsequent as I like.[10]

D. H. Lawrence, declining either actual or artistic involvement in the First World War, employs a Learian allusion to indicate his perception of the conflict as nonsense:

I am not in the war zone. I think I am much too valuable a creature to offer myself to the German bullet gratis and for fun. Neither shall I go in for your war poem. The nearest I could get to it would be in the vein of

> The owl and the pussy cat went to sea
> In a beautiful peagreen boat

—and I know you wouldn't give me the hundred dollars.[11]

Other poets have not simply found Lear worthy of admiration and emulation but have also found him a fit subject for their own verse, beginning with those lines of Tennyson's carved on Lear's tombstone and mentioned by the *Academy* in its obituary notice:

> Illyrian woodlands, echoing falls
> of water, sheets of summer glass,
> the long divine Peneian pass
> The vast Akrokeraunian walls,
> Tomohrit, Athos, all things fair,
> with such a pencil, such a pen,
> You shadow forth to distant men,
> I read and felt that I was there. . . .[12]

Tennyson was writing in response not to a nonsense book but to Lear's travel book, *Journals of a Landscape Painter in Greece and Albania, etc.* However, Lear's ability to make a reader feel "that I was there" applies as much to the geography of nonsense land as to that of the countries described in his travel journals.

A century later Richard Howard, in a poem addressed to the spirit of Wilkie Collins, finds Lear noteworthy as one of a number of Collins's friends whose personal difficulties show through in their art:

> The reek of a "moral hospital," something wrong
> in the nursery, the sickroom, the old men's home:

> that England of your bearded friends who lay blasted
> as it might be like Ruskin and shy Carroll
> by a passion for girls under twelve, like Carlyle
>   by the desperate rant of wisdom that kept him
> from passion at all, like Lear by the "terrible demon"
>   he dared not admit—England was your Native
>   Strain.[13]

Nor are poets the only ones to take Lear as an inspiration. Donald Barthelme has written a brief story, as bizarre in its own way as any of Lear's nonsense, in which he imagines the poet staging his own death for his friends, who, alas, when they come face to face with his idiosyncracies, find him annoying.[14] Lear's drawing style has influenced comic graphic artists like James Thurber and Edward Gorey. Gorey has acknowledged his debt by illustrating editions of "The Dong" and "The Jumblies"; he is one of the few artists who could dare to redo Lear's original drawings without seeming presumptuous.[15]

The finest work Lear inspired, however, and the poem most perceptive in capturing the essence of Lear, was written by W. H. Auden in January 1939:

> Left by his friend to breakfast alone on the white
> Italian shore, his Terrible Demon arose
> Over his shoulder; he wept to himself in the night,
> A dirty landscape-painter who hated his nose.
>
> The legions of cruel inquisitive They
> Were so many and big like dogs: he was upset
> By Germans and boats; affection was miles away:
> But guided by tears he successfully reached his Regret.
>
> How prodigious the welcome was. Flowers took his hat
> And bore him off to introduce him to the Tongs;
> The demon's false nose made the table laugh; a cat
> Soon had him waltzing madly, let him squeeze her hand;
> Words pushed him to the piano to sing comic songs;
> And children swarmed to him like settlers. He became a land.[16]

"He became a land." This line sums up Lear's impact on his readers[17] and perhaps explains the biographical bias of so much that has been written about him. With the possible exception of "The Owl and the Pussy-cat," none of Lear's individual works has a self-enclosed fame. One does not speak of reading specific works, in the way one speaks about reading *Alice in Wonderland*, for example; one speaks of "reading Edward Lear." He and his works merge, become all a part of nonsense land; so just as each one of his works affects one's perception of all the others, knowledge about his life enriches appreciation of the nonsense in a very special way. The case is certainly quite opposite that of the Reverend C. L. Dodgson, whose biography, fascinating as it is, leaves one a bit queasy upon returning to the nonsense composed by his alter ego, "Lewis Carroll." Elizabeth Sewell, after pointing out the numerous similarities between the nonsense of Lear and Carroll, in fact finds in their personalities the primary difference between them, a difference decidedly in Lear's favor: "We are safe with Lear because he is himself safe. . . . The breath of insanity clings about Carroll as it has never done, and could not do, about Lear."[18]

Just as biographical studies of Lear are necessary to show the unity between his nature and the nonsense it spawned, so critical analysis of his poems has as its primary function to show the unity of the nonsense taken as a whole and the necessity of reading it all—and letters, journals, and life as well—in order not to mistake one facet of the Learian paradox for the total picture. A trip to the land that was Lear, what I have been calling "nonsense land," can bring a reader into contact with his own deep-seated anxieties. He will find no final answers to his fears there, but nonsense land somehow lends comfort by the mere fact of containing them. To receive this comfort one must, like Lear, "the Grand Peripatetic Ass and Boshproducing Luminary," travel dedicatedly into the more remote regions. For as S. A. Nock has noted, "whereas Carroll, Gilbert, and others present to the reader a complete, and in some cases almost documented picture of an act which the reader may accept and understand, Lear does hardly more than stir the reader to go adventuring for himself."[19] The critic can only open up the new territories and point out the salient features of the landscape. After having consulted the guidebook, it is up to the reader to take off on further Learian pilgrimages. He will not regret the journey.

Notes and References

Chapter One

1. *Later Letters of Edward Lear*, ed. Constance, Lady Strachey (New York: Duffield, 1911), pp. 135–36.

2. That book was Angus Davidson's *Edward Lear: Landscape Painter and Nonsense Poet* (London, 1938). For speculation on what happened to the lost Lear papers see the preface to the second Lear biography, Vivien Noakes's *Edward Lear: the Life of a Wanderer* (London, 1968).

3. Since early details of Lear's life are sketchy, these mortality figures are approximate. I cite the number of deaths of Lear children in infancy that Philip Hofer gives in the biographical section of his *Edward Lear as a Landscape Draughtsman* (Cambridge, Mass., 1967).

4. *Nonsense and Wonder* (New York, 1977), p. 9.

5. Letter to Emily Tennyson, 10-28-55, quoted by Noakes, p. 130.

6. *Letters of Edward Lear*, ed. Constance, Lady Strachey (London, 1907), p. 148.

7. The Earl of Derby privately published a selection of the results of these years as *Gleanings from the Menagerie and Aviary at Knowsley Hall, Knowsley*, 1846.

8. Incredibly, given their numerous common acquaintances and the detailed records they kept through both diaries and correspondence, the two great Victorian nonsense writers, Lear and Carroll, never met or commented upon having read the work of the other, although it seems unlikely that they did not know each other's books.

9. Quoted by Noakes, p. 119.

10. *Letters*, p. 156.

11. Ibid., p. 136.

12. Ibid., p. 303.

13. As he wrote Fortescue in June 1884: "And, thinking over all, I have long since come to the conclusion that we are *not wholly* responsible for our lives, *i.e.*, our acts, *in so far* as congenital circumstances, physical or psychical over which we have no absolute control,

prevent our being so. Partial control we assuredly have, but in many cases we do not come to know our real responsibilities or our nonresponsibilities, till long after it has become too late to change the lines we have early begun to trace and follow." *Later Letters*, p. 285.

14. Letter to Emily Tennyson, quoted by Noakes, p. 180.

15. See Hofer, *Edward Lear as a Landscape Draughtsman*, for a discussion of Lear's standing as a water colorist.

16. Noakes, p. 178.

17. Lear displayed no false pride about asking his friends for money and to plug his books and paintings; his frankness about his borrowing is one of his most refreshing traits.

18. *Later Letters*, p. 102–03.

19. Noakes, p. 46.

20. *Later Letters*, p. 167.

21. Lear joked that he did not consider himself worthy of full brotherhood in the PRB but regarded himself as a son of the movement. Therefore, he always addressed Holman Hunt, several years his junior, as "Daddy."

22. Lear overheard himself so described by a fellow Englishman while he was staying at an inn during his excursion in Calabria in 1847. Lear good-naturedly adopted "dirty landscape painter" as a soubriquet thenceforth.

23. Reported in *Later Letters*, p. 334.

24. Ibid., p. 333.

25. Ibid., p. 27.

26. Letter to Emily Tennyson, quoted by Noakes, pp. 155–56.

27. Ibid., p. 156.

28. Letter dated 10-15-73, quoted in Noakes, p. 259.

29. Although he never really got along personally with the Laureate, Lear did truly admire Tennyson's poetry. He set several Tennyson lyrics to music and left partially completed at his death a project of illustrating a volume of Tennyson's works to which he had devoted many years of effort.

30. *Letters*, p. 138.

31. Ibid., p. 41.

32. Ibid., p. 104.

33. Ibid., p. 267. The new book, *Nonsense Songs*, did not actually appear until 1871.

34. Lear related the incident to Fortescue in a letter of 10-17-66,

Later Letters pp. 61–63. He retold the story in the preface to *More Nonsense* in 1872.

35. Published in *Teapots and Quails*, ed. Angus Davidson and Philip Hofer (London, 1953), p. 63, which also contains Davidson's remarks.

Chapter Two

1. *More Nonsense*, in *The Complete Nonsense of Edward Lear*, ed. Holbrook Jackson (London, 1947; rpt. New York, 1951), p. 199. All references to the limericks are to this edition. In following notes I will specify whether the verse comes from the *Book of Nonsense* or *More Nonsense* by the abbreviations BN and MN before the page number. Lear's scheme of capitalization of Old Man, etc., alters between these two books. For consistency's sake, when not quoting directly from the text, I will maintain the pattern of capitalization established in the *Book of Nonsense*.

2. There is, to be absolutely accurate, one slight exception to this rule. The limerick in MN about the Young Lady whose nose continually prospers and grows begins, "There *is* a young lady . . . ," p. 175 (italics mine).

3. Thomas Byrom in the first full-length critical study of Lear's poetry, *Nonsense and Wonder*, puts forth several interesting theories about the relationship between the male and female characters in the limericks and about the deemphasis of the Young Lady and the increased security of the Old Man in the second series. He relates the changes from one series to the other to Lear's more settled life and diminished anxieties in the 1870s.

4. BN, p. 40.

5. The final line also frequently introduces a second relative clause.

6. BN, p. 52.

7. MN, p. 174.

8. BN, p. 31.

9. *Edward Lear: Landscape Painter and Nonsense Poet* (London, 1938; rpt. New York: Barnes and Noble, 1968), p. 196.

10. "Nonsense Poetry," in *Shooting an Elephant and Other Essays* (New York, 1950), p. 190.

11. Until Byrom's book and my article "Edward Lear: Eccentricity

and Victorian *Angst," Victorian Poetry* 16 (1978): 112–22 were published, "they" were judged unequivocally as villains.

12. BN, p. 35.
13. BN, p. 57.
14. BN, p. 29.
15. MN, p. 189.
16. MN, p. 193.
17. BN, p. 24.
18. MN, p. 196.
19. MN, p. 205.
20. BN, p. 21.
21. BN, p. 32.
22. BN, p. 46.
23. MN, p. 188.
24. BN, p. 14.
25. BN, p. 55.
26. MN, p. 192.
27. MN, p. 202.
28. MN, p. 180.
29. BN, p. 42.
30. MN, p. 159.
31. BN, p. 55.
32. Byrom, p. 150.
33. BN, p. 20.
34. MN, p. 205.
35. BN, p. 43.
36. BN, p. 50.
37. MN, p. 195.
38. MN, p. 184.
39. BN, p. 3.
40. MN, p. 191.
41. MN, p. 200.
42. MN, p. 169.
43. BN, p. 11.
44. See Byrom, pp. 61–81, for a more detailed survey of "the beasts" in the limericks.
45. BN, p. 23.
46. MN, p. 181.

47. BN, p. 41.
48. BN, p. 11.
49. MN, p. 159.
50. BN, p. 31.
51. MN, p. 171.
52. MN, p. 201.
53. MN, p. 183.
54. MN, p. 165.
55. MN, p. 162.
56. BN, p. 18.
57. Herman Liebert, in *Lear in the Original* (New York, 1975) p. 68, comments also upon the preponderance in Lear of gluttons who meet bad ends.
58. BN, p. 37.
59. MN, p. 182.
60. BN, p. 33.
61. See Byrom, pp. 52–61, for more on music in the limericks.
62. *Edward Lear and his World* (London, 1977), p. 55.
63. MN, p. 192.
64. BN, p. 33.
65. BN, p. 56.
66. Liebert, p. 126.

Chapter Three

1. *Spectator*, December 23, 1871, p. 1571. The reviewer did in fact prefer the limericks to the longer poems.
2. *The Field of Nonsense* (London, 1952), passim. Sewell does consider the nonsense songs as departures from pure nonsense.
3. The arrangement was not, however, intentional. Lear had intended to include limericks in his second volume of poems, but his publisher, Bush, persuaded him to reserve them for a subsequent volume. Perhaps the publisher detected the appropriateness of such a separation.
4. But see Byrom, p. 160, for some darker undercurrents in the poem.
5. The text of "The Owl and the Pussy-Cat" appears in *Complete Nonsense*, pp. 61–63.
6. See Byrom, p. 159, on the sexual confusion. In an unfinished

sequel, "The Children of the Owl and the Pussy-Cat," Lear does make it clear that the owl is the father and the cat the mother.

7. The text of "The Duck and the Kangaroo" appears in *Complete Nonsense*, pp. 64–66.

8. Byrom, p. 164.

9. The text of "The Daddy Long-Legs and the Fly" appears in *Complete Nonsense*, pp. 67–70.

10. Lear had wanted to call the book "Learical Lyrics," which, considering the autobiographical resonances of the poems it contains, would have been far more apt. See Noakes, p. 272.

11. The text of "The Jumblies" is found in *Complete Nonsense*, pp. 71–74.

12. "Die Nonsense-Poesie von Edward Lear," *Neueren Sprachen* 45 (1937): 371.

13. See Sewell, pp. 61–80.

14. The text of "The Nutcrackers and the Sugar-Tongs" appears in *Complete Nonsense*, pp. 75–77.

15. The line contrasts with "They all came back" in "The Jumblies," although *never* is to be the rule in most of Lear's poems.

16. *Complete Nonsense*, p. 21.

17. Ibid., p. 190.

18. The text of "Calico Pie" appears in *Complete Nonsense*, pp. 78–80.

19. Byrom, p. 174.

20. Here I disagree strongly with Byrom, who states that "Mr. and Mrs. Spikky Sparrow" is "a bright, flinty poem, made of tough, trochaic, tetrameter couplets," p. 194.

21. The text of "Mr. and Mrs. Spikky Sparrow" appears in *Compete Nonsense*, pp. 81–84.

22. The text of "The Broom, The Shovel, The Poker, and The Tongs" appears in *Complete Nonsense*, pp. 85–86.

23. The text of "The Table and the Chair" appears in *Complete Nonsense*, pp. 87–89.

24. Byrom, p. 172.

25. *Complete Nonsense*, p. 168.

26. Ibid., p. 194.

27. The text of "The New Vestments" appears in *Complete Nonsense*, pp. 245–46.

28. The text of "The Dong with a Luminous Nose" appears in *Complete Nonsense*, pp. 225–28.

29. The mention of the Bong Tree identifies the Dong's home as the same land as that to which the owl and the pussy-cat travel.

30. Both poems therefore provide an alternative view of the happy courtship of the owl and the pussy-cat.

31. See Noakes, p. 220; Byrom, p. 182; Davidson, p. 197; and Philip Hofer, "The Yonghy-Bonghy-Bò," *Harvard Library Bulletin* 15 (1967): 229–37.

32. Noakes, p. 79.

33. Ibid., p. 95.

34. The text of "The Courtship of the Yonghy-Bonghy-Bò" appears in *Complete Nonsense*, pp. 237–41.

35. There is an unpublished version of "The Pobble" in which the Pobble gives away his toes as a wedding gift to Princess Bink of Jampoodle (printed in Davidson, pp. 241–43). But this version becomes a straightforward love poem. When he decided to stress the loss, Lear eliminated the romantic interest, for loss of love seems to have been the one deprivation Lear could not let his characters convince themselves is for the best.

36. The text of "The Pobble Who Has No Toes" appears in *Complete Nonsense*, pp. 242–44.

37. See Edmund Miller, "Two Approaches to the Nonsense Poems of Edward Lear," *Victorian Newsletter* 44 (1973): 5–8, for his Freudian reading of both versions of "The Pobble."

38. "Sea-green" is the Homeric epithet that Lear adapted as his "pea-green." The use of the original term once again implies that the magic of nonsense land eludes the Pobble.

39. "And all the Sailors and Admirals cried,/When they saw him nearing the further side,—/'He has gone to fish, for his Aunt Jobiska's/Runcible Cat with crimson whiskers!'"

40. The text of "Mr. and Mrs. Discobbolos" appears in *Complete Nonsense*, pp. 247–48.

41. Quoted in Noakes, p. 252.

42. The text of "Mr. and Mrs. Discobbolos, Second Part" appears in *Complete Nonsense*, pp. 249–51.

43. Byrom, p. 203. He also notes the parallels between this poem and "Mr. and Mrs. Spikky Sparrow."

44. The text of "The Pelican Chorus" appears in *Complete Nonsense*, pp. 232–35.

45. The text of "The Quangle Wangle's Hat" appears in *Complete Nonsense*, pp. 252–54.

46. See Byrom, p. 214, for the pertinent examples from the limericks.

47. This list resembles a catalogue of arriving birds in "The Pelican Chorus," but in that verse the departure of the flock also occurs, since that poem describes both coming together and desertion.

48. The text of "How pleasant to know Mr. Lear!" appears under the heading "Self-Portrait of the Laureate of Nonsense" in *Complete Nonsense*, pp. vii–viii.

49. The final lines read: "Ere the days of his pilgrimage vanish/ How pleasant to know Mr. Lear!"

50. *Later Letters*, p. 283.

51. Byrom, pp. 219–20.

52. The text of "Incidents in the Life of My Uncle Arly" appears in *Complete Nonsense*, pp. 275–76.

53. The phrases "the silent main" ("Daddy Long-legs"); "thru the silent-roaring ocean" ("Yonghy-Bonghy-Bò"); "When awful darkness and silence reign" ("The Dong"); and "we stood alone in the silent night" ("Pelican Chorus") all occur in passages describing the protagonist's unhappiness. It is an odd equation, in view of the fact that Lear hated noise.

54. See Noakes, p. 307; Byrom, p. 223.

55. *Later Letters*, p. 283.

56. Byrom, p. 224.

Chapter Four

1. A more balanced view of Lear's nonsense output will be available when Vivien Noakes and Charles Lewsen bring out their two-volume edition of Lear's published and unpublished nonsense sometime in the next few years.

2. See Sewell's *Field of Nonsense* and Susan Stewart's *Nonsense* (Baltimore, 1979). Both authors must use a disproportionate amount of examples from Lear's miscellaneous nonsense in order to bring Lear in line with wider nonsense practices.

3. *Letters*, p. 49.

4. The text of this alphabet is found in *Complete Nonsense*, pp. 131–37. The other two *Nonsense Songs* alphabets follow consecutively on pp. 138–43 and 145–51.

5. The text of this alphabet runs from p. 209 to p. 221 in *Complete Nonsense*.

6. The collective titles may just be a publisher's convention, since the preceding one hundred limericks are designated, conversely, as "One Hundred Nonsense Pictures and Rhymes."

7. One should notice that the parsnip pie is neatly labeled, in the same style as many of the foodstuffs in the limericks.

8. The text of this alphabet is found in *Complete Nonsense*, pp. 263–69.

9. The text of this alphabet is found in *Complete Nonsense*, pp. 270–71.

10. *Later Letters*, p. 58.

11. Ibid., p. 41.

12. *Letters*, p. 8.

13. Lear was fluent in several languages, but Greek, both ancient and modern, was the one he studied and enjoyed reading most intensely. Many passages in the letters are written entirely in Greek, and it is no wonder that so many of Lear's invented words have a Greek look to them.

14. *Later Letters*, p. 60.

15. Both these entries are from the first Nonsense Botany, found in *Complete Nonsense*, pp. 127–29.

16. *The Spectator*, September 17, 1887, p. 1251.

17. The volume's subtitle describes its contents as both nonsense poems and nonsense songs. It seems likely that those less lyrical verses that emphasize language over character prompted the former distinction.

18. The text of "The Two Old Bachelors" is in *Complete Nonsense*, pp. 229–30.

19. This line probably puns on "thyme," a spice that might go well with the sage in a stuffing.

20. The text of "The Cummerbund" is in *Complete Nonsense*, pp. 255–56.

21. The text of "The Akond of Swat" is found in *Complete Nonsense*, pp. 257–59.

22. *Later Letters*, p. 143.

23. See Donald Gray, "The Uses of Victorian Laughter," *Victorian Studies* 10 (1966): 145–76.

24. *Later Letters*, p. 234.

25. Ibid., pp. 235–36.

26. Ibid., p. 263.

27. These names seem perfectly calculated for a nonsense narrative in a mock-pretentious style, but they are the actual names of the four siblings for whom Lear wrote the story. Perhaps audience dictated style.

28. The text of "The Four Little Children" is found in *Complete Nonsense*, pp. 91–106.

29. The text of "The Seven Families" is found in *Complete Nonsense*, pp. 107–21.

30. *Later Letters*, p. 140.

31. See *Letters*, pp. 141–44.

32. *Complete Nonsense*, p. 123. The recipes follow on pp. 123–25.

33. *Later Letters*, p. 119.

Chapter Five

1. *Athenaeum*, February 4, 1888, p. 154.

2. *Edward Lear as a Landscape Draughtsman* (Cambridge, Mass., 1967), p. 59. Hofer does not appear to be aware that the *Athenaeum* obituary is Bryan's probable source of misinformation.

3. See J. T. Brockway, "Edward Lear: Poet," *Fortnightly Review*, n.s. 167 (1950): 334–39, who evaluates the primary virtues the poems convey as gentleness and the innocence of the adult who supports humility and selfless cooperation.

4. Lear's letters contain several passages that describe "beastly" children. Of one little boy, who rebuffed Lear's friendly overtures by commenting on Lear's ugliness, he writes: "It is unnecessary to relate that I turned away with ill-disguised disgust from this offensive infant, who cannot fail to bring his father's gray airs to an untimely hend" (*Letters*, p. 176). And because he had a hypersensitivity to noise, large numbers of children proved trying: "The great drawback here is the noise of the children. There are about a hundred people at meals, and the row of forty little ill-conducted beasts is simply frightful" (*Later Letters*, p. 222).

5. Stefan Kanfer, "Father of the Lorax Turns 75," *Time*, May 7, 1979, p. 93.

6. See my article "Edward Lear: Eccentricity and Victorian *Angst*," *Victorian Poetry* 16 (1978): 112–22.

7. *Hitch: the Life and Times of Alfred Hitchcock* (New York: Pantheon, 1978), p. 31.

8. *Webster's Seventh New Collegiate Dictionary* (Springfield, Mass.: G. C. Merriam, 1972), p. 754.

9. *The Theatre of the Absurd* (New York: Anchor/Doubleday, 1961; rev. ed. 1969), p. 296.

10. "Edward Lear," *On the Margin* (London, 1923), p. 167.

11. Letter to Harriet Monroe, October 1, 1914. In *D. H. Lawrence: Selected Letters*, ed. Richard Aldington (London: Penguin, 1950).

12. "To E. L., on his Travels in Greece," *The Works of Tennyson*, ed. Hallam, Lord Tennyson (New York: Macmillan, 1925), p. 121.

13. "1824–1889," *Untitled Subjects* (New York: Atheneum, 1969), p. 63.

14. "The Death of Edward Lear," *Great Days* (New York: Farrar, Straus, Giroux, 1979), pp. 99–104. My thanks to Marian Rhame for bringing this story to my attention.

15. For further material on graphic artists influenced by Lear see R. L. Mégroz, "The Master of Nonsense," *Cornhill* 157, no. 938 (1938): 175–90.

16. "Edward Lear," *Collected Shorter Poems 1927–1957* (London: Faber, 1966), p. 127.

17. A Mr. Graves, reviewing Lear's three nonsense books for the *Spectator* in September 1887, mentioned a friend for whom nonsense land had become so familiar a place that he composed a list of examination questions about it, e.g. "State briefly what historical events are connected with Ischia, Chertsey, Whitehaven, Boulak, and Jellibolee" and "Enumerate accurately all the animals who lived on the Quangle Wangle's Hat, and explain how the Quangle Wangle was enabled at once to enlighten his five travelling companions as to the true nature of the Co-operative Cauliflower." Quoted in *Later Letters*, p. 329.

18. *The Field of Nonsense*, p. 180. Maurice Baring also derives a favorable impression of Lear's personality from the nonsense: "No one can have read Lear's *Book of Nonsense* without feeling that its author must have been a delightful person," "Edward Lear," in *Punch and Judy and Other Essays* (London, 1924), p. 285. So, indirectly,

does S. A. Nock when he compares one's reactions to the characters created by Lear, Carroll, and Gilbert: "Lear has made of his reader a fellow adventurer, a creator, and consequently a vastly more sympathetic individual then he might be in the company of Lewis Carroll or W. S. Gilbert. Nobody wants to get acquainted with Gentle Alice Brown, nobody has a great desire to meet the Walrus and the Carpenter, but the Dong, and the Yonghy-Bonghy-Bò, and the Jumblies—like Edward Lear himself, they would be welcome anywhere the important things of life are not very important, and where beauty and gentleness are in all things," "Lacrimae Nugarum: Edward Lear of the Nonsense Verses," *Sewanee Review* 49 (1941): 81.

19. Nock, p. 81.

Selected Bibliography

PRIMARY SOURCES

1. Nonsense

A Book of Nonsense, by Derry Down Derry. London: Thomas Mc-Lean, 1846.

A Book of Nonsense (enlarged edition). London: Routledge, Warne, 1861.

Nonsense Songs, Stories, Botany and Alphabets. London: Bush, 1871.

More Nonsense, Pictures, Rhymes, Botany, etc. London: Bush, 1872.

Laughable Lyrics, a Fourth Book of Nonsense Poems, Songs, Botany, Music, etc. London: Bush, 1877.

Nonsense Songs and Stories. Introduction by Sir Edward Strachey. London: Warne, 1895.

Queery Leary Nonsense. Edited by Lady Strachey. London: Mills and Boon, 1911.

The Lear Coloured Bird Book for Children. Foreword by J. St. Loe Strachey. London: Mills and Boon, 1912.

The Complete Nonsense of Edward Lear. Edited by Holbrook Jackson. London: Faber, 1947; rpt. New York: Dover, 1951.

Teapots and Quails. Edited by Angus Davidson and Philip Hofer. London: John Murray, 1953.

"Edward Lear, Three New Poems." Edited by W. M. Parker. *Poetry Review*, June 1950, pp. 81–83.

2. Natural History

Edward Lear's Birds. Collected by Susan Hyman. New York: Morrow, 1980.

Illustrations of the Family of Psittacidae, or Parrots. Published by R. Ackerman and E. Lear, 1832.

Gleanings from the Menagerie and Aviary at Knowsley Hall, Knowsley. Privately printed, 1846.

Tortoises, Terrapins, and Turtles. Drawn from life by James de Carle Sowerby, F. L. S. and Edward Lear. London: Henry Sotheran, Joseph Baer & Co., 1872.

3. Travel

Views in Rome and Its Environs. London: Thomas McLean, 1841.

Illustrated Excursions in Italy. Vols. I and II. London: Thomas McLean, 1846.

Journals of a Landscape Painter in Greece and Albania, etc. London: Richard Bentley, 1851.

Journals of a Landscape Painter in Southern Calabria and the Kingdom of Naples. London: Richard Bentley, 1852.

Views in the Seven Ionian Islands. Published by Edward Lear, 1863.

Journal of a Landscape Painter in Corsica. London: Bush, 1870.

Lear in Sicily. Introduction by Granville Proby. London: Duckworth, 1938.

Edward Lear's Indian Journal. Edited by Ray Murphy. London: Jarrolds, 1953.

Edward Lear in Southern Italy. Introduction by Peter Quennell. London: William Kimber, 1964.

4. Letters

Letters of Edward Lear. Edited by Lady Strachey. London: T. Fisher Unwin, 1907.

Later Letters of Edward Lear. Edited by Lady Strachey. London: T. Fisher Unwin, 1911.

SECONDARY SOURCES

This bibliography does not include contemporary reviews of Lear's works and their later editions. A list of reviews can be found in the bibliography of Thomas Byrom's *Nonsense and Wonder.*

BARING, MAURICE. "Edward Lear." *Punch and Judy and Other Essays.* London: Heinemann, 1924, pp. 255–60. A witty review of Lady Strachey's edition of the letters, coupled with general observations about Lear. Baring points out some howlers involving the editor's mistranslations of Lear's Greek.

BROCKWAY, J. T. "Edward Lear: Poet." *Fortnightly Review*, n.s. 167 1950: 334–39. A sensitive essay that discusses Lear's nonsense as a mixture of tragedy, gentleness, and innocence. The innocence is that of the adult, not the child, because the nonsense creatures display humility and selfless cooperation rather than egotism. The tragedy is that of loneliness.

BYROM, THOMAS. *Nonsense and Wonder: the Poems and Cartoons of Edward Lear.* New York: Dutton, 1977. The first full-length critical study of Lear's poems, viewing them as the poet's spiritual autobiography. Many incisive observations, particularly about the relationship between the illustrations and the poems.

CAMMAERTS, EMILE. *The Poetry of Nonsense.* London: Routledge, 1925. Not a critical treatise on the subject, but an impressionistic reflection upon it, with several interesting comments on Lear's works. Cammaerts defines nonsense as "poetry run wild" and finds it particularly suited to the English temperament.

CHESTERTON, GILBERT KEITH. "Edward Lear." *A Handful of Authors.* London: Sheed & Ward, 1953. General essay with typically Chestertonian analysis of the nonsense.

CROFT-COOKE, RUPERT. *Feasting with Panthers: a New Consideration of Some Late Victorian Writers.* London: Allen, 1967. Chapter 7 considers Lear in the context of other sexually irregular writers of the era.

DAVIDSON, ANGUS. *Edward Lear: Landscape Painter and Nonsense Poet (1812–1888).* London: John Murray, 1938. The first biography of Lear. Not as detailed or accurate as Vivien Noakes's study (see below) but a solid piece of work in which many of Lear's diary entries, letters, and unpublished poems appeared in print for the first time.

EDE, LISA SUSAN. "The Nonsense Literature of Edward Lear and Lewis Carroll." Ph.D. dissertation, Ohio State, 1975. Views the nonsense of both writers as exhibiting an ambivalence between order and disorder, which both use a balanced opposition of form and content to express.

EHRENPREIS, ANNE HENRY. "Edward Lear Sings Tennyson Songs," *Harvard Library Bulletin* 27 (1979): 65–85. General sketch of Lear's relationship with the Tennysons, description of contemporary reactions to his public recitals of Tennyson songs, and details about the publication of twelve of the twenty-one he is known to have composed settings for.

HARK, INA RAE. "Edward Lear: Eccentricity and Victorian *Angst.*" *Victorian Poetry* 16 (1978): 112–22. Deals with Lear's work as it expresses themes common to its age.

HOFER, PHILIP. *Edward Lear.* New York: Oxford, 1962. A handsome pamphlet, designed by John Begg, with illustrations taken from original materials in the Houghton Library and the text from an address Hofer delivered to the Grolier Club in New York City on December 12, 1961. A very general introduction to Lear's life and works.

—————. *Edward Lear as a Landscape Draughtsman.* Cambridge, Mass.: Belknap Press, 1967. A collection of plates of Lear's water color landscapes, prefaced by a long piece on Lear's life, artistic techniques, and the reputation of his paintings from his day to the present.

—————, and THOMPSON, RANDALL. "The Yonghy-Bonghy-Bò: I. The Poem. II. The Music." *Harvard Library Bulletin* 15 (1967): 229–37. Discussion of a holograph manuscript of the poem which notes changes between it and the final version. The second portion of the article considers Lear's musical setting of the poem, indicating how the musical emphases support an autobiographical reading and make the effect of the verse less nonsensical and more melancholy.

HUXLEY, ALDOUS. "Edward Lear." *On the Margin.* London: Chatto and Windus, 1923, pp. 167–72. Brief essay in praise of Lear's poetic qualities. Considers "they" as embodiments of the worst traits of society.

KELEN, EMERY. *Mr. Nonsense: a Life of Edward Lear.* Nashville: Thomas Nelson, 1973. Biographical monograph geared to an adolescent audience. Contains some interesting speculations on how Lear's art shares characteristics of art produced by other epileptics.

LEHMANN, JOHN. *Edward Lear and his World.* London: Thames and Hudson, 1977. An introduction to Lear's life and works for the general reader. Lavishly illustrated, a model of its kind.

LEIMERT, ERIKA. "Die Nonsense-Poesie von Edward Lear (Ein Beitrag zür Psychologie des englischen Humors)." *Neuren Sprache* 45 (1937): 368–73. Defines Lear's attitude, and that of English humor generally, as a sympathetic celebration of the eccentric outsider, of the "solemn fool."

LIEBERT, HERMAN W. *Lear in the Original: Drawings and Limericks by Edward Lear for His Book of Nonsense.* New York: H. P. Kraus, 1975. Facsimile reproductions of the manuscript illustrations of the limericks, with delightful commentary on their absurdities and on differences between the original and published versions of the drawings.

LYONS, ANNE KEARNS, LYONS, THOMAS R., and PRESTON, MICHAEL J. *A Concordance to the Complete Nonsense of Edward Lear.* Norwood, Pa.: Norwood Editions, 1980.

MÉGROZ, R. L. "The Master of Nonsense." *Cornhill* 157, no. 938 (1938): 175–90. Pre-Davidson general sketch aimed at those who know Lear's work only superficially. There is an emphasis on Lear as an artist, as well as a poet, and the influence of his nonsense on later artists and writers.

MILLER, EDMUND. "Two Approaches to Edward Lear's Nonsense Songs." *Victorian Newsletter* 44 (1973): 5–8. The two approaches are to read the poems according to their relationship to nineteenth-century romantic poems (as an escape to a "green world") or to read them as Freudian would. Miller maintains that the Freudian overtones often lead to "ridiculous, rather than sublime, nonsense."

NOAKES, VIVIEN. *Edward Lear: the Life of a Wanderer.* London: Collins, 1968; rev. ed. London: Fontana, 1980. The definitive biography of Lear, making extensive use of his diaries and letters and dispelling some of the myths he created about his family.

NOCK, S. A. "Lacrimae Nugarum: Edward Lear of the Nonsense Verses." *Sewanee Review* 49 (1941): 68–81. A review of Davidson's biography but also a very perceptive overview of Lear's distinctive virtues as a nonsense writer. Sees Lear as "unique in writing in nonsense his emotional biography."

ORWELL, GEORGE. "Nonsense Poetry." *Shooting an Elephant and Other Essays.* New York: Harcourt, Brace, 1945, pp. 187–92. Originally a review of R. L. Mégroz's *Lear Omnibus.* Sees Lear as first true nonsense poet, who writes without satirical purpose and has an underlying layer of sadness. Orwell prefers those works having burlesque elements, dislikes Lear's more whimsical moments.

OSGOOD FIELD, WILLIAM B. *Edward Lear on My Shelves.* New York: privately printed, 1933. Descriptive catalog of Field's large collection of Lear manuscripts and Leariana, much of which is now in the Houghton Library.

PETZOLD, DIETER. *Formen und Funktionen der englischen Nonsense-Dichtung im 19. Jahrhundert.* Erlanger Beiträge zür Sprach- und Kunstwissenschaft, 44. Nuremberg: Hans Carl Verlag, 1972. A broad historical survey of nineteenth-century nonsense literature, exploring the reasons for its appearance and popularity at that time. Examines the works of Lear and Carroll according to comic theory and rhetorical classifications.

PRICKETT, STEPHEN. *Victorian Fantasy.* Sussex: Harvester Press, 1979. One chapter contains a general evaluation of Lear in comparison to Carroll and other Victorian fantasy writers. Some acute observations on Lear's etymological puns in the limericks.

QUENNELL, PETER. "Edward Lear." *The Singular Preference.* London: Collins, 1952, pp. 95–101. General sketch on Lear's works and characters. Views him in the context of other Victorian fantasists who "combined imaginative hardihood with a considerable inheritance of intellectual discipline."

READE, BRIAN. *Edward Lear's Parrots.* London: Duckworth, 1949. Reproduces plates from *Family of Psittacidae* and discusses Lear as an ornithological draftsman. By the expert on this category of Lear's art.

RICHARDSON, JOANNA. *Edward Lear.* Writers and their Work, no. 184. London: Longmans, Green, 1965. Another general biographical monograph, and the least interesting.

ROBINSON, FRED M. "Nonsense and Sadness in Donald Barthelme and Edward Lear," *South Atlantic Quarterly,* 80 (1981), 164–76. Beginning with an analysis of Barthelme's story "The Death of Edward Lear," the author goes on to point out the elements of nonsense, sadness, and escape that the two writers' works share.

SEWELL, ELIZABETH. *The Field of Nonsense.* London: Chatto and Windus, 1952. A theoretical approach to nonsense based on the works of Lear and Carroll. Views the genre as an attempt to detroy all illogical associations in the mind, thus enabling the forces of order to triumph in a game against the forces of disorder. Idiosyncratic, often annoying in its style, nevertheless a thought-provoking work still standard in the field.

STEWART, SUSAN A. *Nonsense: Aspects of Intertextuality in Folklore and Literature.* Baltimore: Johns Hopkins University Press, 1979. An interdisciplinary approach to the genre, highly theoretical and wide-ranging, that uses nineteenth-century nonsense as one of its models.

Index